T0128138

MOSAIC
marriage

Naturally Broken, Discovering Completion

David Barringer

MOSAIC MARRIAGE
NATURALLY BROKEN, DISCOVERING COMPLETION

iUniverse books may be ordered through booksellers or by contacting:

iUniverse
1663 Liberty Drive
Bloomington, IN 47403
www.iuniverse.com
1-800-Authors (1-800-288-4677)

ISBN: 978-1-5320-1349-2 (sc)
ISBN: 978-1-5320-1350-8 (hc)
ISBN: 978-1-5320-1351-5 (e)

Library of Congress Control Number: 2016921181

Print information available on the last page.

iUniverse rev. date: 02/14/2017

To the two who started me on this path by marking the journey with their example. I've followed you as you have followed Christ (1 Corinthians 11:1). I love you mom and dad.

Huge thanks to Harvest Time Partners who have been great personal friends and strategic community leaders. They have been instrumental in helping individuals and families develop strong character.

And character creates opportunities.

www.harvesttimepartners.com

INTRODUCTION

This is a guilt-free book!

This is a collection of memoirs and thoughts. Most of the time, I call them "ramblings."

Call it a mosaic. No specific order, rhythm, or build up. Each chapter is thought for a day; a challenge to work on. There is no precise shape to them. And each one, by itself, contains a component of a greater image.

Just like a mosaic picture it's not about ONE piece, is the accumulation of pieces/moments that make the entire depiction.

This book is here to help, encourage, and build up your marriage (or soon-to-be marriage). It's the guide to marital help one piece at a time.

If you remember anything from this book of musings, remember this: There are two types of marriage

> Those that work on their marriage.
> Those that don't.

From this point on, you are in the first grouping.

And don't ever stop working on it.

PREFACE

I used to run from marriage books. For the first couple years, it was frustrating to read anything about marriage because, quite frankly, I was hard on myself for how bad I was at marriage. I was a workaholic. I was afraid to ask for days off. I was consumed with ministry and neglected what was best. Marriage books and seminars only reminded me what I was doing wrong. I felt I was paying for material that was only going to make me feel worse. I even found myself disgusted with seeing healthy marriages. You should understand: I have high expectations on myself and the type of husband I should be. Those marriages simply made me irritated as I began to compare myself and my marriage with them.

The Problem: I was struggling with "highlight reels."

"Highlight reels" was a revelation that my wife gave me a few years ago. I love highlight reels. As an avid sports enthusiast, they are full of amazing performances that feed my passion and my fanaticism of athletics. By looking at a highlight reel, you can learn so much about a player or a team. What you can't learn from a highlight reel is the whole story.

Case in point, my favorite team: The Detroit Lions (at this time, insert your sympathy feelings for me.) I could show you highlights from the 2008 season. It would be just a handful of plays and ask you how you think the team did. Had you not known the outcome of the season, you'd probably assume they did quite well. Why? You've only seen the "highlights" of their season when in fact, they became the only team in NFL history to lose all 16 of their games. They effectively became the worst team in NFL history.

Anne sat down with woman to talk about marriage. The person she was speaking to said, "I wish I had a marriage like yours. When I look at your Facebook posts, Dave is so encouraging to you and you are so thoughtful." Anne's counsel was perfect.

"Stop looking at highlight reels."

What Anne meant by "highlight reels" was the fallacy of looking at people and trying to get their whole story by looking at the highlights of their lives. A few Facebook statuses do not define a good marriage from a bad one. But we get caught up looking at a few moments in someone's life and we begin to do three things: covet, compare, and collapse.

First of all, to covet means the uncontrolled desire to acquire what belongs to another. We see this develop at the earliest of ages. If you don't believe me, then you need to volunteer in the toddler class in your local church. You'll get a good lesson in "coveting." Case in point, I was talking with a few young families at our church's VBS and noticed a social dynamic developing right before my eyes. The dynamic consisted of a ball the in the hand of a toddler surrounded by 4 other toddlers who had no toy. The look in their eyes made me think of a shark smelling blood in the water. They wanted the ball the little girl possessed. To her credit, she recognized what they wanted and wasn't about to set it down. I watched this battle of wills unfold. You could see the other four thinking through their individual strategies of how they were going to get her to relinquish the prize. As I tuned out the adults, I watched the four do everything within their power to ask, take, and manipulate the little girl into giving up her precious ball.

What seemed to be an hour of activity, really were minutes. And it reflected upon our humanity. As adults, we are no different than those little ones. "Highlight reel" thinking feeds that mindset of coveting.

God, in no way, isn't telling us that we can't desire anything. He is not forbidding ambition. He is not prohibiting us from striving for success. But there's a toxic attitude that creeps in as we begin to envy the "highlights" of another marriage. We begin to think about what we do not possess. It consumes our minds. From there, the coveting begins to sink into our own hearts and bitterness sets in.

Comparisons naturally progresses into coveting. We see the "highlight reel" of someone's marriage and we covet it. We then go home and compare what we saw to what our spouse does. As a faithful watcher of infomercials, I'm always captivated how they show my everyday life and how much time I waste doing life in an ordinary way. So, they offer something that will help me chop, clean, cook, or carry in a more efficient way. To lay it on thicker, they hire actors to act like "every day" people to act surprised and excited as they discover this new-found product. The point: to fill you with envy of what they've discovered so that you make the phone call and set yourself up for 3 easy payments of $33.33.

Someone taught me a valuable truth years ago: You should learn to admire without having to acquire. Why do we compare? Because we've fallen prey to the trap set by our culture. We've gone from impulse buying at the register to getting lost in online auctions and websites grasping at everything we thing we need. Our minds are caught up with how we should look and how we should be perceived by others. We are get deceived with hollow images that have been touched up with airbrushes and manipulated by computer images. Our minds are filled with romantic story-lines that make it impossible to live up to. Comparisons are meant to do one thing: make you and/or your spouse feels inferior. Like walking buy a store window, we glance at another marriage and long for what they have while despising them for attaining what we do not possess.

Lastly, collapse sets in. Our complete make up of mind, will, and emotions were never meant to hold up under the strain of comparing and coveting. Like a table collapsing from too much weight being placed upon it, your marriage will break under the stress of "highlight reel" mentality.

It reminds me of an episode of one of my favorite reality shows where a bar is placed upon the shoulders of the contestants. The opposing team strategically places weights in timed increments upon the shoulders of each individual. Weight upon weight is added to the loads. The viewer knows it's just a matter of time. One by one, contestants begin to struggle under the stress of the weight. Then it happens. One drops from the magnitude of the weight. Like a domino effect, others begin to follow suit. The classic line is heard over and over. "I thought I could last longer."

But that's the deception of coveting and comparing. We think we can last through it. We think we are in total control. Every single fragment of coveting, every time you compare, the "legs" of your marriage begin to buckle under the layers and layers of undo stress. If the load isn't dealt with, it becomes a matter of time when the inevitable happens and collapse sets in. Please understand, I'm not saying this is the place where your marriage is over. I'm saying that you've now positioned your marriage where there are pieces that need to be picked up and fragments to be rebuilt.

Before you continue in this book, I want you to have the release that I needed years ago.

It's the release from having to live…

…the imagined ideal I thought others expected of me.
…the airbrushed-infomercial ideal media impressed upon me.
…the pharisaical ideal I thought my church expected of me.
…the obscenely high-unrealistic ideal I expected of me.

And be (simply said) human. I want to liberate your marriage into the personality what was created when the two of you said "I do." It's being the man and woman God created you to be and learning to live that out, faults and all.

As you read this book, get away from the "highlight reel" mentality with us. Shed it like a snake shedding its skin and leave it behind. We try to get our marriages to live up to an idea we've seen on the big screen or on social media. But marriage is better seen as a mosaic; a complete picture made up of broken pieces perfectly fit together.

In November of 2015, I spent a week in Israel and could not stop gawking at ever mosaic work of art. From the floors of grand cathedrals to wall coverings depicting tales from the past, the intricacy of this craft captures our imaginations. Why is this artistry so captivating? Each fractured piece of material that is used has its own history. Its own story. On its own it may not be remarkable but when all the shards of material are brought together in a particular way, it tells a greater, more beautiful story.

There is nothing perfect about marriage. It's full of flaws and issues. We carry into it shards and pieces of our background and personality. But when it is put it all together in a covenant with God, a beautiful picture is depicted.

It's easy to see what may be wrong. Up close, you'll see bits of imperfection. But if you stand back you'll see an image only made complete in Christ.

Anne and I do not have a perfect marriage. Personally, I think it's a great marriage. Nevertheless, it's a marriage that's full of flaws and issues. Why? Because we are two broken individuals that came together and made a covenant before God and man. This book will tell of moments that make up the whole of who we are. Each experience we have had brings its own story. But put it all together, the shards of experiences and memories, and a beautiful picture is depicted. The stand too close to us you'll see bits of imperfection. If you stand back, we hope you'll see an image only made complete in Christ.

We are a mosaic STILL being put together. And so is your marriage.

Contrary to the movie Jerry Maguire, we didn't "complete each other." We are two people that have found our completion, not in our marriage, but in our faith Jesus Christ. He's been the source of peace, strength, comfort, joy, and hope.

And it's because of Him, we've enjoyed 18 years of marriage and many more to come.

So, this is where we start. This is where everything begins.

2 Broken people; 1 complete couple.

A Mosaic.

- 1 -

"Happy Wife; Miserable Husband": 6 Reasons Why Appeasement Doesn't Work

You've said it, I've said it: Happy wife...happy life. Call it nice. Call it sweet. I call it appeasement. It's a conflict avoidance style that sacrifices your feelings, beliefs, or ideas in order to pacify or please the other person. To some, this seems like a noble identity to assume. After all, keeping peace and harmony in the relationship is important. But, is "giving in to get along" an effective method for fostering a healthy marriage?

Nope.

Appeasement has never been an effective strategy in marriage (or parenting, or friendship...or, well, life). Don't get me wrong, it's good and gracious to be accommodating to the preferences of your husband/ wife in various circumstances. Our first response should always be to serve. In strong marriages, both spouses understand both give and take. Servanthood is a mark of healthiness. But when one spouse ALWAYS GIVES and the other ALWAYS TAKES major problems are unavoidable.

Constant yielding to your spouse may appear to achieve the desired peace, but this peace, at best, is temporal and superficial. In reality, appeasement brings eventual harm to the marriage.

Here are some of the reasons why...

1. **Replaces Christ as the center of the relationship.** Instead of a relationship that pleases the heart of God, all actions are done to please the heart of the spouse being appeased. It's through him we are created and he holds all things together (Colossians 1:17 ESV)

2. **Creates a one-sided relationship.** Constant appeasing one's spouse will empower him/her to assume a position of dominance in the relationship. Appeasement makes one spouse inferior to the other. This creates an imbalance that will fracture the oneness that marriage was designed by God to be. (Mark 10:8 NLT)

3. **Removes the word "no" from your marriage.** I've found that couples that have an issue with appeasement want to say "no" but just don't know how to say it properly. "No" is a very good word and keeps us in check. Healthy marriages don't look to say "no" but are not afraid to say it in a healthy edifying way (Romans 14:19 NLT). Without "no," the whims and desires of the spouse are controlling the relationship.

4. **Removes respect.** I find both the spouse that is appeasing, and the empowered spouse\, lose respect for one another for different reasons. The lack of healthy servanthood erodes the opinion that each spouse as of the other. Romans 12:10 (NLT) says to "take delight in honoring." Appeasement keeps you from doing that.

5. **Cultivates a spirit of fear.** Appeasement replaces the heart of serving the needs of your spouse is with the anxiety of having to constantly attend to the wants (not necessarily needs) of the spouse. That mindset will loom over the marriage creating an atmosphere that God never designed us to live in. (2 Timothy 1:7 NLT)

6. **Develops frustration.** The appeasing spouse lives with unmet needs. He/she represses heartfelt feelings at the expense of legitimate needs. Unfulfilled needs tend to re-emerge and manifest themselves in other ways – depression, anger, bitterness, resentment, regret, and so forth. Appeasement literally drains the joy of serving your spouse. (Galatians 6:9 *"Words kill, words give life; they're either poison or fruit—you choose." Proverbs 18:21 (The Message)*

Appeasement doesn't work. Like scratching poison ivy, it feels good in the moment but spreads faster than you intended to places you never wanted it to go. I'm not a proponent of shifting to the opposite of appeasement (which is domination...basically involves one or both parties striving to have their desires prevail).

But appeasement will feel right in a moment but will erode what you are trying to build.

Marriage is a daily walk of humility before God and our spouse. Don't stop serving each other. Be willing to take a step a step back and ask yourself, "How full is the 'love" tank of my spouse? Have I been more of a taker than a giver?" If we'll be humble and honest as couples, we'll see stronger and more fulfillment than we dreamed of while showing an example of Jesus to the world around us.

- 2 -

The 2 Things I Got Right in Marriage: Thoughts for Singles (also married peeps)

Anne has been on me a while about writing a marriage blog to singles. I've been setting aside the idea for a long time. But over the past two weeks, some comments have come my way,

"I love reading about your mistakes. They help me correct my own."
"Some of your mistakes help me to know what to NOT look for."

So, I've been asking myself a simple question: Of all the things I've done wrong (the list keeps growing), what have I done right?

I came up with two.

That's it.

Obviously, there's more, but these were literally the first TWO that came to mind that, I believe, are the TWO FOUNDATIONAL decisions that has given me a great (not perfect) marriage. Again, I've gotten other things right in the past 18 years, but they've built off these two.

If you're single, this is where you START.
If you're reading this and your married, this is what you WORK ON.

The **FIRST** thing I got right: I loved Christ before I loved Anne. There is no other foundational decision greater than this. Everything, and I mean everything, builds off this. Let me explain. In Matthew 22 (MSG), Jesus was asked about the greatest commandment. He said,

"'Love the Lord your God with all your passion and prayer and intelligence.' This is the most important, the first on any list. But there is a second to set alongside it: 'Love others as well as you love yourself.' These two commands are pegs; everything in God's Law and the Prophets hangs from them."

I cannot possibly love Anne the way she needs to be loved without first loving Jesus. I've had people take offense to that type of priority. But when I love the Lord first, He teaches me how to love.

Why is that? When I encounter His love, it teaches me how to love myself AND others. It helps me live life through His perspective. I forgive completely because that's how He forgives. I have compassion for others because He showed me compassion. I serve selflessly because He served me by laying down His life. I choose to love unconditionally because He chooses to love me that way.

I'd love to say I've perfected all but, as you've read in previous blogs, you know I'm a work in progress as are all of us. But this is where I start from and CONTINUE to build on. Any season that I face, this is where I begin. And it's given me a powerfully healthy perspective to have.

The **SECOND** thing I got right: I chose a woman who loved Christ before she loved me.
I didn't ask her for an application followed with references and a dissertation. I saw her devotion to Christ.

When worship began, she entered in as a passionate worshiper.
When someone was in need, she gave without expectations.

When something needed to be done, she was the first to serve. When someone needed to be encouraged, Anne was the first to step up. But most of all, her reputation amongst people who knew her was the reputation of Jesus. She had the character of Christ (Galatians 5:22-23 NLT).

She's nowhere near perfect. Like me, Anne has plenty of flaws and it's not my place to list them (that point may be for a future blog). It's my place to see her how Christ sees her. And that list what I saw. Her life was evidence of a Matthew 22 life. I knew if she loved Jesus completely, she could love me that way (because I'd love her that way).
If you're single, this is where you start. Instead of trying to find the "right one" for you, become the "right one" for others. Go after Matthew 22 passionately. As you encounter the love of Jesus, it'll change you AND change what you look for in a spouse.

If you're married and you didn't start this way. Don't scrap everything. Start a Matthew 22 marriage today by letting the love of God change you. And from you, let His love encounter and change your marriage.

I love you all. I believe in great things for you. Why? Because I know how great Christ is and I know, through you, great things can happen.

- 3 -

"The Try"
10 Ideas to give a "try"
in your marriage

My wife married a sci-fi geek. I'm not ashamed of it. I embrace it. Anne, not so much.

In his endeavor to become a Jedi, Luke finds himself needing to get trained by the best. It is here we get one of the most well-known figures in all the Star Wars universe: Yoda.

For us geeks, his wisdom pours out in a fantastic line that is just as iconic as the character,

"Do or do not. There is no try."

I've heard it used and stated in so many different contexts. Why not? It's an amazing piece of wisdom used to motivate his young apprentice to take some actions-steps forward. A few days ago, I saw it tweeted in regards to sex in marriage. My immediate first thought:

Discouraging "trying" may not be the best marriage advice I've seen. So, I thought I'd do the opposite. I want to encourage "trying." Why? For the couple going through struggles, it's the personal effort the two of you need to show each other. It's the extra "try" that screams "I'm not giving up...we're going to make it."

For the couple going through a season of life where you feel you're just "existing" together. No fights, no scuffles, yet there is no fun and no passion. The "try" just may catapult you forward over the hump into an amazing season of refreshing.

For the couple in a good place in life, the "try" can be an extra log to the fire. The time to try something new and exciting isn't when things are getting mundane or frustrating. That's the worst time to try to get momentum. The perfect time for the "try" is when things are great. The momentum picks up and flows. Makes me think when scripture says, "from glory to glory."

Here we go, 10 things I want you to "try" in your marriage...we'll start with a few simple BUT powerful tips but please don't tell yourself "I'm not going to "try" to do any of these unless I'm in the mood." It's time to back away from what you need step up into the "try" for the sake of your spouse and your marriage.

1. **Try to smile.** Sometimes we save our smile for our kids, friends, and/or for the people at church. We take our smile for granted when it comes to our spouse.

2. **Try to complement/encourage.** Sometimes we resort to "I'll do it if he/she does it." Or I've even heard this one, "He/she doesn't deserve it." Childish tendencies take over us sometimes. What brings it out? Hurt. This is a basic need in EVERY human. Hebrews 3:13 (NLT) says to "Encourage each other daily." If you don't do this for your spouse, the enemy will use someone else to fill that need and NO ONE should out-encourage/complement you. Step up and try it.

3. **Try to surprise.** Get spontaneous. I'll admit, my wife's version of surprise is different. She likes to know what it is before it's "sprung" upon her. That way, she can prepare her OCD self for it and actually enjoy it. I can't push my style of surprise upon her and expect her to enjoy. Find your spouse's love language and get out of the rut.

4. **Try prayer and devotions.** I know what you're thinking: "Shouldn't you have had this at #1?" I'm a pastor and I thought you'd expect that. Some couples, like me and Anne, have a hard time with doing

"couple devotionals." We tried it and it didn't fit. But the key is this: we tried it. Now, we'll pass on to each other books, blogs, and sermons as we look out for the spiritual well-being of the each other. I love putting my arm around her at night and praying over her. I love hearing her pray for me. Our devos may be separate, but it's morphed into us pouring into each other in a way I didn't expect. But it happened with the "try."

5. **Try nudity.** (I thought that would get your attention.) We base so much of sex as a "mood" or "an act." For those that push "the act" upon the other, you ignore the emotions/mood. For those that are all about the "mood," you ignore this necessary and beautiful act of marriage. Bring the "try" into your bed. Why? It's humility; You're not there for "you." Try sex from the vantage point of your spouse. The bed isn't there to meet your needs; it's there as a platform to meet your spouse's needs. Remember this: there is NO ONE else in the entire world that can meet this need in your spouse. It's you.

6. **Try a date.** Most couples know that dating each other is necessary... well, kind of. This is so simplistic yet I find it's completely ignored and taken for granted. It doesn't have to be expensive. It may not have any cost for that matter. Anne and I like the simple walks together. We've even taken our kids on walks. The point was to have time together (which is Anne's love language...that and Swedish Fish). Try it. Ask your spouse out. Plan the day/evening. Pour into their love language.

7. **Try to listen.** A friend of mine gave me a quote I've used on my kids and I've needed to use in marriage. "Listen to me with your eyes." Eye contact speaks so much to the person talking. It shows more that singular focus. It shows you are valuing them and their voice. Proverbs 20:12 (NASV) says "The hearing ear and the seeing eye, the Lord has made them both." Get past "Elevator talk" in your marriage. Your ability to actively listen conveys the value your spouse needs from you.

8. **Try to forgive.** The preach in me wants to just say "Just forgive. Make yourself do it." But I felt the Lord leading me to challenge you to "try" forgiveness. Why? So many people are afraid to "try"

it because of how it may be received and/or given. Colossians 3:13 (NLT) challenges us to "try"/step-out into it regardless of your spouse's reaction. The response of your "trying" isn't your responsibility. The forgiveness is.

9. **Try to be healthy.** I know we're 'merica. We're a nation of unhealthy activities with unhealthy food. But this shouldn't be our excuse to develop healthy hearts, bodies, emotions, and spirits. I'm not asking you to be a marathon runner. I'm not demanding you to become a vegan. I'm asking you to take an honest inventory of your life and ask yourself, "Where can I get healthier?" The bible says, "the two become one." If you are actively "trying" bringing health into your marriage (God's word, healthy relationships, healthy food, exercise, etc), you are setting your marriage up for potential success.

10. **Try** _____. This is where you must get your imagination going. It's about you knowing your marriage and trying something that may be new or it could be something that needs to be revived. Get creative. Talk with your spouse. Go after something today.

Yoda had it wrong. "Do or do not. There is no try." And unfortunately, so many people don't/won't try. This needs to be a new habit for this new year. Don't wait for you to be in the mood to "try." If that's the case, it'll never happen because it's about you. Get humble and get "trying."

Sometimes it isn't really about the "what." Sometimes all that matters is that you "tried."

- 4 -

Elements of an Effective Date in Your Marriage Part 1
"Avoid Elevator Talk"

"Date nights" were of such an extreme importance for most of us before we were married. It's where we learned everything we needed to know about our spouse before we married them. The problem: we got married only to find out we didn't know as much as we thought we did. He snores, she makes a weird sound when she chews, he hums while he pees, she squeezes the toothpaste from the middle instead of the end... there's so much of life we didn't grasp in our pre-marriage date nights. For some reason, couples stop frequent dating once the honeymoon is over. I've heard all the excuses, "We been married _____ many years, we already know everything about each other" or "he/she knows how I feel." Oh, if only, as we age, we stayed the same and our likes/dislikes remained unchanged.

Pre-marriage dating was meant to bring us together. Why do we stop dating once when we are married? Did we reach a point of knowledge saturation where we no longer have a need to be closer to our spouse? With the divorce rates, I believe circumstances demand post-marriage date nights.

Element #1: Avoid "Elevator Talk."

You step into an elevator intending to go to the 5th floor. After a couple of floors, someone steps onto the elevator with you. What do you talk about? Most likely, the weather is the most common thought of topic of conversation and it lasts just 20-30 seconds...just long enough to fill the awkward silence till the 5th floor is reached. You walk out breathing a sigh of relief that the moment is done and you can get going about your day.

Sad to say...that just described the approach some people have with their spouses and one of the reasons they don't want to go out on a date. "What will we talk about?" "We like different things?" "What if he/she talks about something I'm not interested in?"

What's crazy: We didn't worry about that before the ring. I want to restore your faith in your conversational skills. For couples who stopped talking, it's not that you stink at communication, it's just that communication skill has not been exercised and used. Just because I took German for 3 years in school 20 years ago doesn't mean I'm fluent in it. I stopped using it and it's grown weaker. You have to exercise your communication.

Of all the things that go on in a date, why start with "communication"? Because communication is the oil in the engine of the date. You can have any restaurant or atmosphere, but without any type of conversational connection, it's nothing more than a "hang out"...and two strangers can do that. Let us help with a few things we've learned.

Dating Conversation Do's and Don'ts:

Do keep eye contact. If you (like me) can't handle ESPN being on the TVs and keep eye contact, don't go to that restaurant. Your eyes reveal that you are engaged in the conversation. Your spouse wants to know that your attention is fixed upon them and your date. Proverbs 20:12 (NASV) says, "The hearing ear and the seeing eye, the Lord has made them both." (from Anne) Lock eyes and show your interest. Learn to be a listener with your eyes.

Don't unload. If you're on a date, it's time for you two to engage and interact. A date isn't the time to unload anger and frustration. That should be taken care of in your home communication. If your dating is always filled with heavy "unloading", either one or both of you will NOT want the date in the first place.

Do find ways to engage. (from Anne) That means you are other-centered. Find ways to interact in the stuff your spouse is into. They know you may not fully care about what they care about, but you asking and engaging speaks volumes. A verse I refer to a lot is Philippians 2:3 (NIV) "Rather, in humility value others above yourselves." For example, Anne doesn't give a care about sports, she cares about me. So, periodically, we'll be on a date and she'll see something sports-ish and ask me about how my teams are doing. Deep down, I know she doesn't really want a breakdown of the NFC North, but I means the world that she'd ask.

Don't "one up" your spouse. "I had a rough day" gets followed up with, "Your day couldn't have been as bad as mine." We, for some reason, have an issue with someone being happier, more talented, or even more miserable than ourselves. "I broke my nail today" is followed by "Oh yeah, I broke my finger." It's ridiculous. (from Anne) But so often we demean our spouse and what they are trying to convey by dwarfing their experiences with our prideful approaches.

Do practice "good" conversation. Make sure that every time you two go out, your conversation should be uplifting, edifying, and enjoyable. You don't want it weighed down with gossip, slander, and bitterness. Again, dates are meant to deepen your understanding of each other not of someone else's business. Proverbs 15:23 (MSG) "Congenial conversation—what a pleasure! The right word at the right time— beautiful!" Ditch the heaviness of destructive conversation and walk away from your date healthy because you chose to practice healthy conversations.

Don't let dating conversation be your only marital communication.
Your dating conversations will be disastrous if this is the only time you talk to each other. It's like saying, "We're married, living together, but we ignore each other throughout the week till date night." There should be constant, healthy marital communication being fostered throughout a normal average week. Good everyday marital communication will produce GREAT date communication.

Do truly listen. (from Anne) Don't try to hurry your spouse up so you can talk about what you are wanting to talk about and tell "your thing." Listen to what he/she is saying. What emotion are they invoking? What does their body language say? Do their tones tell you something different from the words being spoken? I love what James says in James 1:9 (NLT) "let every person be quick to hear." Be quick to step up your listening skills by being an active listener. Be in tuned to everything being communicated by your spouse.

Don't stop trying. Everyone struggles with conversations. The more changes that you and your spouse go through, and we all change, it can get easy to take the other for granted and just, well, not date AND communicate. Keep talking. Keep trying.
Dating is huge in marriage. But it's hard to date with ZERO to little conversation going on. Set the date. Get the baby sitter. Go out and enjoy an evening of ZERO elevator talk and engage with your spouse.

Elements of an Effective Date in Your Marriage Part 2 "Get the right atmosphere."

Have you ever come home to a house where the atmosphere wasn't what you thought it was? After a great day at work, I've walked in the door noticing something about the atmosphere of our home. As I'm walking up the stairs into our living room, I say to myself, "there's something in the air tonight." The place is quiet. There's tension in the room. Nobody is talking or moving. I come to find out there had been a "disagreement" between my wife and my daughter. What was a pretty joyful day, has now been transformed to guarded tension. I'm not sure what happened, but the atmosphere sets the tone and mood for any events and/or plans.

Atmosphere is sorely underestimated. One of the many things I learned yesterday at a conference was setting the tone/atmosphere of a room before communicating. It not only gives you a platform to communicate the necessary information but aids and/or guides what is being said as to be as effective as possible. As much as this works in sermons, presentations, conflict, and child-rearing, it is essential in marriage...specifically today in our conversation on dating our spouse. For you scientific peeps, atmosphere (thank you Wikipedia) is a layer of gases surrounding a material body of sufficient mass that is held in place by the gravity of the body. Earth's atmosphere, which contains oxygen, also protects living organisms from genetic damage by solar ultraviolet radiation. For the non-scientific peeps, atmosphere is simply a covering of gases to protect life and help life to survive.

(Just stick with my "nerdy-ness" for a second...it will all make sense.)

Atmosphere has three characteristics:

1. **It protects.** The atmosphere guards us from harmful things form the outside as well as keeps a healthy climate for growth.
2. **Sustains life.** Atmosphere provides air for plants and animals to breath. Without it, there is no life.
3. **Multi-layered.** Earth's atmosphere is broken up into five layers. Each layer carries its own purpose and function.

Carrying and caring about the atmosphere of our post-marriage dating is no different from those three characteristics. Especially if you are the one planning the date, it is vital you establish "atmosphere." Don't underestimate it. Don't overlook its importance. It will set you up for dating success or failure.

Can we get EXTREMELY practical with this?

Think about it...**providing a proper atmosphere for dates with your spouse...**

1. **Protects your time with him/her.** If your marriage needs a quiet night out where you two need to talk and reconnect, and you chose to go to Buffalo Wild Wings during a Monday Night Football game, the atmosphere will destroy what you set out to do (it would work for me). Yet, if you two need to go out for a fun evening of activity and laughter, a quiet candlelight dinner may not conducive to protect what is needed for your marriage. **The atmosphere sets the tone for the evening and protects what is needing to happen on your date.** This is easy as doing some simple steps:

- Plan ahead. Spontaneity is okay. But some spouses stress over some details. Take stress out by planning.
- Plan what to wear and communicate it. If you're heading to a comedy club and she's dressed for a fancy dinner, it'll ruin the night.
- Talk about what to expect. Build some anticipation with your spouse. Get excited about the date.
- Be other centered. Plan the evening so that you are not the beneficiary of the entirety of the date. Avoid the location/activity that you most want to do.

2. **Sustains the life of your marriage.** Dates should be places to catch your breath. But more than that; **they are places to get fresh breath into you.** Some people don't take this seriously. "We don't have time to date...we have kids/jobs/responsibilities." I will say in response: **you make time for the things that are important.** Just as much as the physical atmosphere provides air for plants and animals to breath. Your atmosphere of post-wedding dating will do the same. During the date, it will breath into your marriage...
- The priority of your spouse.
- Selflessness.
- Dedication to a healthy marital relationship.
- A resurgence of intimacy.
- A healthy view to your children. They will see and reproduce it in their future marriage.

3. **Dating atmosphere is multi-layered.** What I mean by that has nothing to do with the exosphere or the troposphere. It has everything to do with knowing that **one type of atmosphere doesn't fit EVERY date**. Anne and I do a variety of stuff. Why? We have a variety of needs. Sometimes we go to a movie. Early in our marriage, we'd get Taco Bell and walk through a furniture store (yep...you read that right...we like looking at furniture). The more you communicate, the more you'll see that a careful care of your dating atmosphere will maximize your dating experience.

For the guys reading this, I'm not saying it'll promise more sex (even though that's never a bad thing), but it promises a profitable dating experience.

You need to keep the atmosphere multi-layered. Don't do the same thing all the time. Shake it up.

- Go out and laugh.
- Absorb a moment together.
- Take a walk through a trail.
- Do something you used to do before you got married.
- Find a place to make-out. (just checking to see if you were paying attention...but hey, you're married! Who's gonna argue?)

I've always been very passionate about the Psalms. In Psalms 63:3-5 (MSG), the writer pens his feelings about the atmosphere that God provides. "You've always given me breathing **room**, a place to get away from it all, a lifetime pass to your safe-house, an open invitation as your guest. You've always taken me seriously, God, made me welcome among those who know and love you."

I know that I cannot provide the proper atmosphere for my wife without knowing and experiencing the atmosphere the Lord provides. Why do I know what to provide for my wife? I learned it from Jesus. His presence is a place for me to "breath" and "a place to get away from it all." I just take what He has shown me and I pour it into my marriage. Sometimes I miss the mark. Sometimes I screw up. But effort and passion help provide a great base of building a great dating atmosphere.

Provide an "atmosphere" for your dates. Provide that place that will protect and sustain your husband/wife. Let them be blown away what is "in the air tonight."

- 6 -

Elements of an Effective Date in Your Marriage Part 3 "Turn up the romance."

Romance is more confusing than we realize. The second we assume what romance is, something changes. It could be the season of life, it could be her/his tastes have changed, or it could be your approach has NEVER changed and, therefore, predictable and unromantic.

Most couples were very romantic during dating/courtship. It's there that romantic expressions are usually at their highest. For many reasons, our desire for those expressions diminish greatly after the honeymoon phase of marriage. Some of you reading this believe romance isn't as necessary as it once was. You believe it isn't or shouldn't be as important as it once was. I think romance expressions is what adds the fun and adventure to what can be an otherwise predictable routine of life. Please understand: Marriage cannot survive purely on romance. But it is a very important part of a healthy marriage. And this is often the first thing lacking when a marriage becomes boring.

It's why I've come up with a simple definition of romance: Selflessly serving your spouse's love language. Love languages are not only diverse, they change depending upon the season of life you are in. Therefore, romantic expressions are diverse. Romance depends upon the person receiving the action and not necessarily the person giving it (that's an important thing to realize). To one couple may be as simple as a thoughtful note left on the dresser, unexpectedly helping with chores, or an evening out so no one has to cook or clean the mess. But it should also include a regular date and a weekend getaway (when the budget allows for it).

To help with your understanding of romance...
Romance cannot:

- **Make areas of conflict disappear.** Romance doesn't turn you into the Houdini of conflict.
- **Change your spouse.** You can't use it as manipulation to form your spouse into the person you want.
- **Subsidize growth areas.** Romance can't take the place or cover up areas you need to grow in.
- **Solve your marital problems.** Flowers doesn't take away what you said about her mother.
- **Doesn't guarantee more or better sex.** It's not a magic spell that's been cast over your spouse to ignite an insatiable libido. (I know what you're thinking after that last one..."what in the world is romance there for?")

Romance has a deeper purpose to it. **Romance can:**

- **Assist you in connecting in a completely different plane than what everyday life provides.** It breaks you from the norm and allows you to get out of the rut of the ordinary.
- **Rekindle and reminds.** Romance gives you the reminder you need. It's remembering your life and love before the responsibilities of marriage set in.
- **Usher in the fun and laughter that's necessary.** Couples that frequently laugh together don't get divorced. Romance lets you have fun and laughter together.
- **Build your friendship with your spouse.** Romance creates a depth to your relationship/friendship because it is other-centered.

- **Increase intimacy.** Disclaimer: Intimacy does not equate to intercourse. But as the same time, I highly encourage couples to increase intimacy both in and outside of the bedroom.
- **Creates memories.** What you don't want to hear is, "Remember when you used to..." Romance helps create new memories and moments.
- **Sets the stage for open and honest communication.** Which can obviously lead to the resolution of conflicts, deeper conversions, greater date nights, and better sex.

Marriages without romance are empty and, in my opinion, kind of boring. Understand: **they are not boring me...they become boring to the people involved.** Being bored in marriages is cancerous. The marriages that I have witnessed make a priority of dating are marriages that have a greater capacity to facilitate health. In those marriages, there is a high expectation of romancing their spouse. It doesn't mean they're a specialist at romance. You don't have to be skilled at it. It's all about the heart and the effort.

I scripture that have kept going back to Revelation 2 (ESV). Here, the words speak out to the church in Ephesus, "repent, and do the works you did at first." Ephesus was a church that was doing good works but they were falling out of their passion for God. The words given, "do the works you did at first." In other words, do the things you did when you first discovered your passion for God and rekindle that relationship. Just as it works in our relationship with God, it works in our relationship with our spouses (marriages reflect God...but that's for another blog). Take your marriage and "do the works you did at first." I want to encourage you: never let the romance die. It is an important aspect of cultivating your relationship/friendship, and shouldn't be tossed aside as unnecessary.

When was the last time you enjoyed a romantic time together? A romantic surprise? A romantic anything? Plan to do something special this month and see if your marriage doesn't benefit. You will most likely feel a bit awkward if you haven't done this in a while. BUT DON'T LET THIS STOP YOU! Find out what speaks to your spouse. Find out what he/she wants to do. Get spontaneous. Get creative. Don't worry about failing at being romantic. Your effort and heart will show through.

- 7 -

"Foreplay is Always in Play."

Honor marriage, and guard the sacredness of sexual intimacy between wife and husband. Hebrews 13:4 (MSG)

From the get-go of this blog, please note: The goal isn't to get more sex into your marriage (though I'm not against that whatsoever). The goal is to develop intimacy. Sex doesn't necessarily lead to intimacy. Intimacy doesn't always involve sex.

I had heard a teaching years ago about premarital sex. I was a teenager, I was in church, and words were being used in church that most people would thing shouldn't be used (probably what shaped my blunt approach). Then the teaching went the issue of foreplay. From my limited understanding and zero experience, my ears perked up, and yet, I kept wondering, "should I be hearing this? Is it okay for me to know about this?" I felt dirty for being there. The uneasy feeling, I had, wasn't due to the material being taught. It was my misunderstanding of how God views sexuality between a husband and wife. He created it for marriage to be indulged in AND enjoyed. Why don't we say that more in church? Why isn't that taught more? I thank God for the parents, youth pastors, leaders, and mentors in my life who had the guts to speak the truth of God's word into every area, especially sexuality. It's given me the freedom and boldness to teach, preach, talk, counsel, and blog on this vital area to marriage.

For the life of me, I cannot remember who was teaching/preaching that day 20+ years ago, but I do remember him redefining the word "foreplay." Two of his points where as follows: (paraphrased) 1 - Physical touch grows and 2- Foreplay goes beyond the bed. I'm gonna do my best to do this justice...

First, the physical affection you entertain and indulge in were designed to bring a growing connection. It wants to go further. The term I coined is "**progressive connection**." A kiss, hug, a holding a hand, all done in the proper way, should leave the thought, "I'd like that to happen again." Teenagers (in my day) would say, "We took things too far and things just happened." Well of course something "happened." Physical affection, without standards or limitations, was designed to progress forward. We are designed by God as sexual beings. There's nothing dirty about it. In fact, scripture says, you were "fearfully and wonderfully made." But like all things God designs and gives, there is a stewardship of it. (Parent Note: Don't be ignorant. Guard what you see your kids doing with their boyfriends/girlfriends. What they do in public, they'll take it a step forward in private.)

Secondly, foreplay doesn't just happen in the bedroom. **Foreplay is the daily courtship of the heart** and, therefore, not limited to a bed. It is the accumulation of moments; the buildup of passion. Call it a "snowball effect." That means, if properly handled, it can be fostered over the course of a day/week instead of trying to "jump-start" it in a moment (not that I'm against "heat of the moment" times for marriage... go for it). If we can wrap our minds around that, it would dramatically affect our marital sex life. It'd remove the idea of "intimacy is just for a moment" into the place where **intimacy is how we live**. If husbands and wives can see the simple everyday moments are ALL foreplay, our approach to our spouse would forever be changed. It may add more sex (no promises), but I guarantee it will add more intimacy.

Here are 6 ways to rethink everyday encounters with your spouse:

Greetings and Goodbyes. Monitor how you leave the home and how you return. The way you send off your spouse into their day should make them smile instead of relieved you're gone. The way you return or what he/she returns to shouldn't make him/her wish they'd stayed at work a bit longer.

Reconnections. How you keep in contact throughout the day is a huge deal. Even if you're not a cheesy romantic and slip notes into the pockets of your spouse, casual texts and phone calls matter. This is where social media can be a huge gift. Tweet to your spouse. Message him/her. Take a pic of the meal that's ready. Text something sensual to him/her (hey your married...nothing wrong with that unless a coworker picks up your phone and looks at it. Be careful).

Fighting well. Skirmishes happen. It's inevitable with two humans living together in matrimony. But fight fair and in a healthy way. Don't go for the selfish win. Go for marital win. Fighting from a place of humility doesn't seem normal. It's because it isn't. Intimacy flows when pride is laid down.

Releasing poison. How you handle forgiveness can revolutionize your marriage. I've heard it said, "Unforgiveness is the poison you drink that you think will kill someone else." Withholding forgiveness might be strangely satisfying as if you're making someone suffer for what they've done. But it's slowly killing you and your marriage. Watch your attraction increase with the poison of unforgiveness flushed from your system.

Selflessly serve. This does two things. First, it makes you look for your spouse's love language and, second, fosters humility. Meet your spouse's needs without the need for reciprocation. In other words: True serving has no strings attached. You serve regardless of what you get back. Imagine a marriage where two people are, daily, looking for ways to serve the needs of the other spouse.

Safe touches. A UCLA study showed that human beings need 8-10 meaningful touches a day. Learn to touch with zero expectations. 67%

of men have "touch" as a dominant love language. But, because they haven't exercised stewardship over their love language, they don't know how to exhibit physical touch without their wife thinking they're only doing it for sex. Introduce (or reintroduce) "non-sexual" touch. It's touch without sexual expectations. Hand holding, massages, a (light) slap on the rear, embraces, etc. should be active in regardless of the years of marriage. There should be adequate and appropriate touches enjoyed.

I love what Hebrews 13:4 (MSG) says, "Honor marriage, and guard the sacredness of sexual intimacy between wife and husband." I think that part of honoring and guarding "the sacredness of sexual intimacy between wife and husband" is making sure that we are courting their heart and passion in a way that serves them. And serving isn't done by one single act. It's a lifestyle. We saw in Jesus when it came to his bride, the Church. He served regardless of what he received. He gave knowing we could never reciprocate that level of giving. How much more should we strive to build into our day, intentional actions to serve our spouse? I promise, courting their heart can revive the passion back into your marriage.

Don't leave foreplay in the bedroom. It wasn't meant to live there.

- 8 -

"Say No to Venting"
6 Ways to Appropriately Deal
with Marital Frustrations

I'm a pro social media guy. If you follow me, you know I post just about everything. I try to keep most of my tweets/posts about things that are edifying or of comedic value. But as you well know, social media is a breeding ground for venting. One my personal pet peeves on social media is a venting post with zero ability to be constructive and ends with, "just sayin'."

It's always the quandary I find myself in as a pastor. I've drawn certain boundaries in my posting when it comes to my opinions about issues. My choice in those boundaries help me to not walk with reactionary posting but to carefully chose what represents me.

In the name of free speech, we blast people, political parties, sports teams, and churches. We harness the right to post what we want without wondering if it's right to do it. I understand the need to talk things through (my afternoon and evenings are filled with appointments like that). But I'm afraid in the name of "venting," we've done more damage to our marriages than helping them.

A great rule of marriage communication is this: **Never talk badly about your spouse to other people or vent about them online. Protect your spouse at all times and in all places.** Your marriage is (should be) the closest human relationship you have. If it's not there (yet), then being a "protector" instead of a "vent-or" (not really a word) is a great place to start building health back into your marriage. Don't run from conflict. Face it in a healthy way and watch God bless your marriage.

Instead of venting about your spouse, here's some help on appropriately dealing with your spouse.

1. **Go to the source of the offense before you go to sources of venting.** Matthew 18 (ESV) gives us a great start to dealing with people who have offended us (especially our spouse). If your spouse is the source, go to him/her first.

2. **Keep your communication open and clear.** The words "open and clear" make us keep in mind that communication is more than verbiage. Like good plumbing, keep blockages from the flow of communication by removing what will clog up what you are trying to convey. For example:
   - Attitudes have to be adjusted.
   - Timing must be appropriate.
   - Mannerisms and countenance must give a disposition of healthy confrontation instead of attack.
   - Keep others and their opinions out.
   - Clothe yourself in humility.

3. **Don't build up support.** It's easy to find people to rally to your side AND you know who they are. They're getting your side of the story and that's not okay. You're presenting a one-sided argument to them and they're biting the hook. Protect your spouse by making sure that he/she isn't going to feel ganged up on. When you back someone into a corner, they come out swinging and end up doing more damage out of pure survival instincts. Keep your biz between you and your spouse. (Don't forget that rallying family to your side is just as, if not more, damaging.)

4. **Protect your spouse.** People like to offer their opinions (especially family members). Opinions get offered but they don't need to

be accepted. You may be hurting in your marriage, but protect your spouse. The entertaining of negative rants, bad attitudes, and ignorant rants are toxic to your heart. Don't tolerate it. Why? What you don't deflect, you will reflect. What you reflect, you will ultimately embrace. Step away from the toxic stuff and protect your spouse.

5. **Seek appropriate counsel.** Appropriate counsel is someone who...
   - ...will objectively look at your situation without letting friendship/relationship dictate direction.
   - ...will NOT just tell you what you want to hear. He/she must be willing to have the tough convo with you.
   - ...will lean upon Biblical principles and not emotional decisions.
   - ...will recognize there is another side to the story. (Your perspective isn't the only perspective in the situation.)
   - ...will depend upon the Holy Spirit for direction.
   - ...will breathe hope and not distress into your life.
   - ...will have the guts to call out unhealthy behaviors.

My final thoughts go to an amazing narrative in scripture found in 1 Samuel 14. Jonathan is looking to move forward into conflict. Traveling with him is his armor-bearer. The armor-bearer could have asked to stay behind and refused to go with him. But his reply is priceless, "Do all that you have in mind," his armor-bearer said. "Go ahead; I am with you heart and soul." 1 Samuel 14:7 (NIV)

We need spouses who are willing to approach battles/conflict "heart and soul" with each other. It's a decision that is done as individuals as well as a couple. But to you reading this...let it start with you first. Be the first one to step up and proclaim, "I am with you heart and soul."

Conflict is inevitable. We are a broken people living in a broken world which means that life can take us through some sucky situations. But we have a Savior who is an overcomer. He is with us "heart and soul." And if "God is for us, who can be against us?" If our overcoming God is with us, there isn't an insurmountable situation he cannot help us walk through...heart and soul.

I believe the best is yet to come for your marriage.

Keep trusting in Christ. Keep walking in healthy marital habits.

- 9 -

"Flirtationship:
3 Steps to Keep Flirting in Marriage"

"Give honor to marriage, and remain faithful to one another in marriage..." Hebrews 13:4 (NLT)

For a while, this blog has been developing in my heart. I know that the potential of it can create a firestorm of responses of emotion and opinion. If you don't know me well, my heart is always of compassion driven by the love of Christ. I do not blog out of a place of judgement. I write out of a position that strives to stay humble and teachable before God as I recognize my life AND my marriage is a continual mosaic being formed by the Holy Spirit.

My heart is for healthy marriages and to help encourage practices that help build marriages...
...AND to help identify those practices that are destructive to couples.

Flirting is a topic you don't hear much about as something detrimental to a marriage. I think part of it is the glamorization of it in most entertainment. It's just accepted as something men and women "just do." The sensation of catching the eye of someone else, the flattering feeling of receiving attention from someone, and the thrill of being pursued by someone is what we see amplified. You're living in a flirtationship; you're more than just a friend but less than a full-blown relationship. What you think is innocent, is really deteriorating the intimacy of your marriage. Flirting should only be reserved for your marriage.

Flirt verb \'flərt\ 1. to move erratically 2. a: to behave amorously without serious intent b: to show superficial or casual interest or liking Notice the words, "to behave amorously." It means with a sexual or intimate desire without serious intent. Over and over I've heard people say,
"It was harmless flirting."

Now some would say that I may be blowing this out of proportion, but is not flirting generally the first step towards developing romance, as this is what singles usually do to signal interest in others? When I was single, flirting was about catching the eye of someone else. It was taking a chance to make a contact. The contact was intentionally laced with the potential of a next step (connection, date, relationship, someday marriage). I can't say I was the best "flirt" as a single. I didn't have the pickup lines or the smooth conversational styles. (Sometimes I wonder what Anne saw in that awkward 18-year-old.)

But can we just admit that we all know what flirting is and not cover it up with flashy words or excuses? I don't think we need to debate it. We could argue about whether it's intentionally wanting sex or not, but that's not the point. The point is that we know flirting is about creating intimate connections. And when we are creating intentional intimate connections with people outside of our marriage, we are flirting with marital disaster. It's why Jesus warned us about our thought-life and the way we look at others that are NOT our spouse in Matthew 5:27-28 (NLT)…

"But don't think you've preserved your virtue simply by staying out of bed. Your heart can be corrupted by lust even quicker than your body. Those leering looks you think nobody notices—they also corrupt."

Flirting with someone other than your spouse VIOLATES…

- Honor: It removes the "worth" from your marriage. It takes the priceless attention and affection reserved for your spouse and directs them elsewhere. The sensuality of our hearts should always and completely be directed toward your husband/wife.
- Trust: It develops a two-sided heart as you are splitting it between your spouse and whoever you are flirting with. And it is difficult to trust a spouse who has one eye on you and another eye on someone else. NOTE: Flirting also develops a lack of trust in yourself. The rush you can get from flirting is addictive. Thus, this next point...
- Desire: It confuses your senses. Why? Because flirting focuses on what is easy about the relationship (attraction) and not the hard work that makes it work. Desire is closely related to...
- Vision: It seduces you to think you are missing something in your relationship and/or makes your marital struggles look larger than reality. It seeds a false sense of discontent. Instead of putting more effort into your marriage, it's easier to focus energy into others who are outside of your relational strife.
- Thoughts: Flirting with others invites them into your thoughts and fantasies. You begin to play "what if" and before you realize it, the passion begins to die down as you slowly disengage from your spouse without even realizing it.
- Faithfulness...Why? Flirting doesn't want to stay stationary. It wants to grow. Again, is flirting not what we did before marriage as to create an inroad into a potential relationship? Can flirting be done without action? Maybe for a season. But what is allowed to grow inward WILL manifest itself on the OUTWARD.

How does a marriage avoid "Flirtationships?" Try these 3 simple steps:

1. Keep your spouse's love tank filled. I'll never give a free pass to anyone starting a "flirtationship." But a great way to prevent one is to keep the "love take" of your spouse filled. Most "flirtationships" I've dealt with (most that ended in an

affair) started with one person having a void in their heart. Their spouse didn't fill it. Again, it's not an excuse, but an explanation. Don't give the Devil a <u>place to tempt</u>. Find out what their love language is and DAILY speak it. Think of it like a glass. If you keep it full, there's no room for anyone else to add anything. Which leads to #2...

2. Flirt with your spouse. What I love about the scriptures is when it is silent on a subject, it's saying something. If it is NOT silent on something, it's screaming something. When it comes to our intimacy and sexuality (which flirting is a part of), we have parameters of keeping all sexuality in our marriage. Within the marriage, the silence of scriptures give us creativity (thus the <u>Song of Solomon</u>). Do ANYTHING you feel you'd like to do to catch the eye of your spouse (as long as it's safe, legal). Get creative BUT make sure your kids are guarded so they don't get scarred from the "dirty" text you sent your husband. :)

3. Be cautious of admonition. I believe that Christians should be the most encouraging people around. You can give compliment without sexual connotation. You can offer a nice sentiment without anything suggestive. BUT if it's being received as anything BUT admiration, then back away, dismantle any mistaken expectations, and inform your spouse of the misunderstanding. It will build trust between you two. Of all the temptations, anything that is of intimate in nature, scripture tells us to flee from them (1 Corinthians 6:18 ESV).

As Hebrews 13 (NLT) says, "give honor" to your marriage. Hold it in high regards by keeping your attention and affection completely to your spouse. Be creative with it and re-find the joy in the pursuit of flirting with your spouse.

I believe in you. I'm praying for you.

- 10 -

"Assaulted with Assumption"
5 Marital Assumptions to Deal With

It only took me 5 or so years, but I discovered that Anne wasn't the biggest fan of flowers. It's not that she doesn't like them (she confirmed she did), but they didn't speak to her ANYTHING close to what I thought they were communicating. Through dating and into marriage, I had been buying them thinking that was speaking the value I assumed they were communicating.

Yep...not so much.

I wasn't necessarily hurt by the truth about the flowers. I was more ticked off I realized how much money I spent in 5 years of roses when it could have been used for something like an Xbox...er...something for our marriage.

Assumption has made fools of us all. It's like a carefully hidden spider web laid out to catch unsuspecting individuals casually walking by. Unfortunately, too many couples find themselves caught and tangled up in it. It can lead to frustrations and, if not corrected, fracture in your relationship.

When it comes to my marriage, what shouldn't I assume?

1. **Assuming my spouse knows that I love him/her.** "My spouse knows how I feel" is not a statement of marital strength as it is

the admission of relational laziness. The longer you've been with someone the more apt we are to take them for granted. To add more fuel to this fire, if we don't recognize/know their love language, the few times attempts get missed because he/she wasn't looking for and/or doesn't operate with that specific form of communication. I'm not advocating annoying your spouse with reminders like a paranoid maniac, but there should be a balanced frequency to the communication of the passion you have for your spouse. Appropriate and balanced communication creates a connection that is essential to the emotional and mental health of your marriage.

Action Step: From random texts to the way you end conversations, find strategic and consistent ways to remind your spouse how much you love her/him.

2. **Assuming things are fine as long as there aren't any big problems.** Whenever I ask premarital couples about the definition of "big problems," I always hear the same answer: adultery. Certainly, that's a significant issue. But marriages get fractured and fall apart on far less. It's said "it's the little things that matter." Most of the time we think "little things" pertain to the small touches for an event (date, birthday, anniversary). But the "little things" also have to do with those habits we've have been trying to learn to live with. It's those frustrations you thought would just go away and/or you would just get used to. From under-appreciation and lack of quality time to chronic complaining and gradual physical distancing, fracture has one goal: complete brokenness.

Action Step: At an appropriate time and place, sit and have an honest talk. You may worry about feelings getting hurt, but revealing frustrations in a healthy conversation is constructive. Letting them go is destructive.

3. **Assuming your spouse values what you value.** You didn't marry yourself. You married a different human being which means

you will likely have different values. Anne and I have the same value of what makes a restful vacation but have different values in what constitutes a "clean" house. The goal isn't to get the two of you to fight it out to have the same values, it's to, first get you to appreciate your differences, and second, to work together so marriage embraces both of your values. So many couples struggle not because someone isn't unwilling to bend/change. It's because there hasn't been any "value" brought to what your spouse values. This is a huge point of frustration that leads to a cloudy home atmosphere.

Action Step: Sit and evaluate the areas where the two of you differ. Don't assume you know how the other feels about what you value. Be willing to understand his/her point of view and, possibly, make some changes.

4. **Assuming how my spouse is feeling about our relationship.** Just because you haven't heard any complaining doesn't equate to having a spouse with complete marital satisfaction. That's like thinking because you don't see the oil light appear on your dashboard means you don't need to check it and/or get it changed. I recognize some don't ask out of fear of what they are going to hear. Ignorance is not bliss. And the time to ask is NOW. You may not want to hear you might be missing the mark on an area or two, but knowing what to work on will give your life marital tread in moving forward to see health in your relationship.

Action Step: Take up the habit of asking your spouse, "Is there anything that I can do to be a better husband/wife?" Don't wait until something blows up to realize that what you're dealing with could have been avoided.

5. **Assuming things will never change.** This breaks my heart EVERY time I hear it. It's the cry of hopelessness and stubbornness. It's the permission we give ourselves to give up. Hebrews 6:19

(NLT) says, "This hope is a strong and trustworthy anchor for our souls." Having Christ as the central element of our marriage hasn't kept our marriage from storms. But our hope in Him has given us an anchor in them. If you have Christ in your life, then you have abundant hope.

Action Step: Walk in humility, servanthood, and boldness. It doesn't mean you become a doormat to your spouse. It does mean that you first initiate change in your own life, and second, you are looking to foster hope by being the catalyst of change in your relationship.

Is there anything should I assume? Absolutely.

Assume the best in your spouse.

Put your hope in Christ and look at your spouse through the lens of Jesus. See your spouse the way Christ sees them. Stop thinking the worst about them. Refrain to let your mind and emotions put your attitude into a place where you're living hopeless and constantly frustrated. The reality is: Christ never stopped his pursuit of us despite our issues. Neither should that stop us.

Set your hope in Christ and let the hope see the best in your marriage.

- 11 -

"A Marriage of Mistakes"
18 Lessons Learned from
18 Years of Marriage

Today is my 18-year anniversary...
(just caught something as I'm typing...Let me start over.)
Today is OUR 18-year anniversary. Outside of encountering Christ, May 23, 1998 was the greatest day of my life. But in the midst of the roughly 6,570 days of marriage, I've made a few mistakes. Mistakes are fine; they happen. Anne didn't marry perfection nor did I. But the goal is, if there are mistakes, and there will be, is to try to not make them again.

So, I thought what better day than our 18th anniversary to list out, for educational purposes, 18 mistakes we've learned from (that hopefully you will learn from too).

1. Stop comparing with other couples. They are not you.
   o I believe that you can GLEAN ideas from another couple; just don't think you need to duplicate who they are.
2. When your wife goes into labor, don't make her wait to leave for the hospital so that you can unhook and bring your PlayStation.
   o BONUS: Don't tell her you're bringing the PlayStation because you "don't want to be bored." That's a whole other mistake.

3. Assumption is cancerous to the unity in your home.
   o Assumption the devil's workshop. If you're going to assume ANYTHING, then always assume the best.
4. Don't sneak up on your wife purposely because you think that scaring her will be funny.
   o It'll never be funny…. never!
5. Devaluing your wife's idiosyncrasies devalues her personally.
   o God created each of you with idiosyncrasies none better than the other. They are a part of your personality.
6. When your apartment is on fire, while she is grabbing the wedding photos and irreplaceable items, don't grab the PlayStation.
   o Things can be replaced. (Yes, I have issues and am getting help.)
7. Couple's devotions don't work for Dave and Anne.
   o We both felt guilty for not doing them. The guilt lasted till we realized that we both have the same elements to a walk with Christ, but we do them differently and at different times. It doesn't stop us from looking for moments to pray over each other, but we've felt a release of having to do everything the same in our journey of following Christ. Our steps may not look similar, but the steps will always be together.
8. Don't demand what your love language craves.
   o Serve first. Give first. Speak her love language first. Let your serving lead to reciprocal giving.
9. Refuse to try changing your spouse.
   o Pray that God would BLESS her and CHANGE you. Let the Holy Spirit do the changing and quite trying to play his role.
10. Always offer the last of the ice cream so that, according to scripture, "it may go well with you."
    o I may have taken that scripture a bit out of context but 'yall know what I'm talking about.

11. Anne doesn't have to like sports.
    o   My spouse liking what I like is not essential to a happy marriage. Our differences in leisure, hobbies, and overall personality adds to the makeup of our marriage; it doesn't take away from it.

12. The silent treatment might be the stupidest way to communicate anger.
    o   I'm good at it. And as a professional in it I can confirm that it doesn't work and does more damage than you desired.

13. I wish someone would have told me how to have a "time out" during disagreements.
    o   Instead of throwing a chair (early in our marriage), stepping away to calm down and remember what's important would have been a far more constructive decision. My blow-ups created more casualties.

14. Snuggling is fun for moments, not the entire night.
    o   It sounds good, and I'm a physical-touch guy, but you gotta have your own space at some point. It's the only way to get some solid sleep.

15. If I'm after a win for "ME," it'll never be a win for the "WE."
    o   If the win isn't for the marriage, it'll never be worth the price of victory.

16. I don't "babysit" my kids. I don't "watch" the kids so that my wife can go out and have a token evening with her friends.
    o   I'm their father. I spend time with them because I love them, I need time with them, AND they need time with me. Also, your wife needs some sanity away from the kids. Plan a father/kid evening in your weekly/bi-weekly schedule.

17. Grudges rob more time than you want and consumes more of your mind than you'll ever anticipate.
    o   "Will you forgive me" and "I forgive you" may be the 7 most powerful words you and your spouse can speak. So, speak them often.

18. It's not a sign of weakness to ask for help; it's a sign of weakness to NOT ask for help.

    o   Anne and I are very thankful for the men and woman who have, and continue, to speak into us. We haven't "arrived" yet. There's still a lot to work on

I'm capping it at 18 (having made more mistakes than this list can contain). But I love that practices what the Apostle Paul taught us,

Make allowance for each other's faults, and forgive anyone who offends you. Remember, the Lord forgave you, so you must forgive others. Colossians 3:13.

Love ya babe! Thanks for letting me "ramble" for the past 18 years...

- 12 -

"Hungry Hope"
4 Ways to Begin a Culture
Hope in Your Marriage

"This hope is a strong and trustworthy anchor for our souls..." Hebrews 6:19 (NLT)

Hope seems like it's such an elusive element in marriage today. Couples, typically, feel they either have it or they don't. But as this blog has been brewing in my spirit over the past couple weeks, I've recognize that the internal struggles so many marriages are experiences may stem from an incorrect view or understanding of "hope."

At risk of sharing too much of my message for Sunday at Kfirst (I'm preaching on hope), wanted to speak to this amazing, yet seemingly illusive element, into your marriage.

Scripture tells us, "This hope is a strong and trustworthy anchor for our souls..." Hebrews 6:19 (NLT)

This writer of Hebrews tells us, better yet, encourages us, that "this hope" is not grounded in our abilities. Better said: we can't create hope. It is something offered through the work and power of Jesus.

Having said that, it should change our view of hope. Instead of seeing as something we have to manufacture, perhaps we need to see it an ethos, or atmosphere to be nurtured or strengthened. Hope is always available in Christ. Hope is always there. But practically lived out, I find it in one of two states: We are either feeding an ethos of hope or we are starving our marriage of it.

I love my former pastor. Joel Stocker is one of the greatest mentors in my life and, quite simply, I feel like I owe him so much. He has given me a fresh outlook on being a pastor, restored joy into ministry, and has given me a great example to follow. I have a lot of stories about Joel.

One of my favs was a video I got to see of him. The back story: Joel would go camping on a yearly basis with several his friends. One of the sources of pride and joy was the "immense" fire he would build for the entire group. His 2 key elements: a ton of wood and diesel fuel (it burned cleaner is what he told me).

This one instance, a few friends snuck to his site and replaced his diesel with water. That evening (on the video), he built his traditional fire and began to pour the "fuel" on the wood. With everyone gathered around watching (and in on the joke), he tried to light his kindling. The kindling caught a bit, but not much. "Pour more gas on it" people yelled. So, he did. Long story short, Joel successfully built a campfire with wood he was personally dousing with water. When he found out the joke, the look on his face was priceless.

My take-away lesson from my mentor: Desire and effort far outweighed the suppressant.
Let's just be real. Normal life can drain hope. Family moments, social media, work situation, conflict at church, political climates, etc. all can suppress and/or completely stifle hope. You don't need to look for an excuse for no hope. The excuses are everywhere. And it's easy to think you don't possess it because of what surrounds you. And if that is what you are feeding off, it's of no wonder why life seems so hopeless.

I never want to belittle someone's situation. I have never been in your shoes (nor do I want to) and you have never been in mine. Let's all keep our own footwear on and own up for our own lives. **But, in marriage, this is where you and I need to make TWO conscious decisions:**

1. **Will I try to manufacture temporary hope or will we choose to embrace hope in Jesus?**
2. **Will I choose to feed the ethos of hope or starve it?**

The silly story about my mentor is such a valuable parable of what our response to hope should be: This broken world of natural "hope" suppressants, we need to rise above it (desire) and take the responsibility (effort) to feed it.

Like it or not, **if you are not feeding "hope," you're feeding something else.** Take your pick, despair, anger, resentment, cynicism, etc. all are bottom feeders that will find sustenance off hopelessness.

My simple, and practical approach: Cut off what is stifling the flames. Push past the feelings of hopelessness and foster an atmosphere of hope.

How do you feed hope? It's more simple that anyone will give it credit for.

1. **Put your trust in Christ.** All your efforts will amount to a shallow semblance of hope that has no lasting power. He is the source of hope. He is the foundation to build a culture of hope in your marriage.
2. **Be the first to act.** As much as I want you as a couple to do this together, so much hopelessness and despair is grown because of stubborn attitudes. Don't say the words, "I won't unless he/she does it to." Be a forerunner. Set the pace. Initiate the atmosphere of hope.
3. **It's a daily decision.** Dedicate yourself to it. It doesn't come from a one-time act. You can't turn the Titanic on a dime and your

marriage issues. Purpose in your heart that hope is just as valuable to your marriage as breathing is to your body.

4. **Don't despise small beginnings.** An ethos of hope is fed in the seemingly small little moments and decisions. It's in the simple things like:

Don't let anyone out-encourage your spouse.

Show acts of kindness toward him/her.

Find a way to serve your spouse's love language.

Walk in generosity as a couple. Find a way to give.

Get naked with your spouse.

Find a ministry to serve in together.

Do a service project as a couple/family.

Pray for and/or with your spouse.

None of these are "quick fixes." But they're a creative and practical start. Find ways to feed hope.

As said before, **if you are not feeding "hope," you're feeding something else.** Let that ethos start with you. Instead of praying for God to change your spouse, pray for God to change you. Be the change your marriage needs. And the beauty of hope is it doesn't come from you. It's anchored in Christ. But you do have the responsibility to foster that culture of hope in your marriage.

Blessings on you. Feed hope. Let the ethos (culture, atmosphere) of hope transform your marriage.

- 13 -

"Broken Trust"
8 Ways to rebuild trust back
into your marriage

He heals the brokenhearted and bandages their wounds Psalm 147:3 (NLT)

Trust is a necessary element and is the foundation of every healthy relationship. In fact, trust is the security that makes intimacy possible in marriage. Like an organism, it must be nurtured and not ignored. My dad taught me years ago.

"Trust is like fine china; it's beautiful to have but it can be broken quickly. And to fix it, it takes a lot of time, effort, and patience to put it back together."

That's stuck with me for years. I don't know any other accurate way to describe the value and fragility of trust.

I've never met a relationship that hasn't encountered difficulties with trust. I would even argue that most difficulties in relationships stem directly from a breach of trust. I'm not saying everyone has had devastating circumstances, but we all have had moments where trust, on some level, has been compromised.

Marriage requires strong trust. So, I'm giving you a list that may give you a few ways to build it (or rebuild it).

1. **Trust does not equal forgiveness.** Forgiveness and trust are two different things. When you've been wronged, you should give forgiveness instantly (which is "Grace"), but you should build your trust slowly. Forgiveness by its very nature cannot be earned; it can only be given. Therefore, we forgive the way God forgives us: instantly. Trust by its very nature cannot be given; it can only be earned...built. For that, it takes time and effort (reference the opening illustration about the cup). Forgiveness has to come first and then grace can pave the way to restoration and renewed trust.

2. **Stop dancing around the subject.** Be open and honest. Take responsibility. "The devil made me do it doesn't work." Healthy steps forward begin with complete and utter transparency. The offender must own his or her sin without any "yeah-buts." It's not okay to say, "I'm sorry I hurt you and let you down, but . . ." It's never okay to rationalize or justify sin. Ever. The only way to rebuild trust is to take full responsibility for our actions. Period. It's also critical for the offended person to do some self-assessment as well. Broken trust is rarely 100% the other person's fault.

3. **Humility is king.** We love to cover up the embarrassment of our faults. Don't be defensive, righteous, or casual about the problem. It's nothing more than a smoke screen trying to distract away from what needs to be dealt with. There must be a sincere heart as well as honest effort to work out the issues. If you are the one who is at fault, the more defensive/righteous/casual you are, the less you are able to hear what your spouse has to say, and the worse their hurt will get.

4. **Don't obsess.** Whether you were wronged or you were the perpetrator, take steps forward by letting go of the past. When you obsess over each insult, each act, each thing done wrong – you are not giving yourself time to heal from it. You need to heal in order to begin to trust again. If you're hurt by your spouse's actions, work on releasing and moving forward. Living in the past continues to open

the wound. If you're the one who did the hurting, stop fixating on your fault. If God has forgiven you and your spouse has forgiven you, then you need to forgive YOU.

5. **Accountability; Be an open book.** That means open your cell phone, calendar, email, and social media to your spouse. (Free Marriage Tip: Anytime you are feeling the need to hide something from your spouse should be a red flag...unless it's a surprise birthday gift.) Accountability is usually the hardest part. Why? People feel entitled to privacy. The problem is that smacks against the "oneness" that marriage is called to operate in. Be willing to temporarily give up some freedoms. At this point, you will need to take a moment and ask yourself what is really important: your relationship or your privacy? It really comes down to that.

6. **Patience and hard work.** Time doesn't heal everything but it applies to every part of the healing process. Just as you can't make a wound on your arm heal, you can't make the heart heal overnight. A gift doesn't make the hurt go away. Sex doesn't make the problem disappear. You need a patience heart, listening ears, and intentional and consistent actions that will aid in the rebuilding of trust. Set some goals. Work on them together. Review the results and reward the efforts (not the results).

7. **Practice the three "A's" daily: Affection, Attention and Appreciation.** Communicate with words and actions to your partner how much you love and appreciate them in big and small ways every day. Speak in their love languages and help them understand you are desiring health and healing. If you are the offended, your spouse feels like a failure and you do NOT want to keep them there. If you are the offender, make sure you stay engaged with your spouse. Let them know you are a trust-builder more than a trust-breaker.

8. **Get some help.** Don't be afraid to seek out counseling with a trusted advisor whether it's a marriage counselor or a pastor. Even though it's easy to get help from a friend, you need to find someone who is non-partial and as some wisdom to speak some Godly wisdom into your marriage. Make sure the help is for the both of

you. (Another marriage tip: avoid involving other family members because it can exacerbate the situation.)

I return to our opening scripture,

He heals the brokenhearted and bandages their wounds Psalm 147:3 (NLT)

I believe everything we do in life should model who God is. He is the healer of brokenness. He doesn't leave us in a fractured state. And just as God moves toward us in that manner, we should model that in every area of our life...ESPECIALLY our marriage.

Be a rebuilder of trust. Bind up the brokenness in your marriage. Be known as a healer...just like our savior is.

- 14 -

"Pants On Fire"
5 Steps to dealing with
lying in your marriage!

Truthful lips endure forever, but a lying tongue is but for a moment.
Proverbs 12:19 (NIV)

Marriage is a covenant. A promise.

In our wedding vows, trust is both explicit or implicit. It permeates the commitment we make to our spouse so that we can start off from the foundation of trust both in Christ and in our spouse.

Trust is one of the most essential elements to an intimate relationship. And without it, we are sentencing our marriage to a future of frustration and fracture. It doesn't mean trust is not restorable. A marriage can recover from broken trust AND survive for the long-haul. But it takes patience and hard work from both spouses do see that healing take place.

Of all of the components that can fracture trust, lying may be at the top of the list.

People lie for numbers of reasons. Insecurity. Pride. Anger. But to boil it down, people lie to protect themselves. Many times, it begins when someone is experiencing shame however trivial it may be. Why? It seems easier to lie than it is to face confrontation. But that's where lying becomes like a drug. Lying sedates the moment while making you a slave to its agenda: Total destruction.

Why do people lie?

1. Because there's something to hide. People lie to protect interests. There seems to be little care about other people's feelings in the matter. The actions are selfish and destructive. Where scripture challenges us to "walk in the light." Lying wants to remain in the shadows.

2. Because people feel they can—it works for them. Liars are convinced they'll get away with their lie and never get caught. So the fib continues until they discover that this is not working for them and a new lie must be spun. You end up in a prison of falsehood with an identity you cannot live up to and bondage you cannot escape from. It's why Proverbs 19:5 says, "he who breathes out lies will not escape."

3. Because people believe they have a right to lie. "I'm doing this for the good of my marriage!" People will use lying as if it's the only way to bring health. But what they're really doing is utilizing lying to manipulate the situation bring their intended results. They're prayer has gone from "thy will be done" to "my will be done."

4. Because it makes a person "look better." It a form of pride. Lying takes control of the narrative so that it doesn't center around what God desires but what he/she desires. It ignores Matthew 6:33 so that I seek "me" first and add God later.

5. Because habitual lying has developed serious character problems. Lying sears the conscience. The more you indulge in it, the more apt you are to listen to your lie than the leading of the Holy Spirit. Lying desensitizes our spirit so that our character takes on the falsehood of our facade instead of the image of Christ.

"What do I do if I find out my spouse is lying (regardless of how big or small it is)?"

1. Pray and seek wisdom. Seek the Lord's help. Get wisdom from a trusted counselor (not necessarily a friend/friends).
2. Bring what is in darkness into the light. Recognize the pain involved. Removing a splinter doesn't feel good. But you know, at some point, it has to come out. And the longer you wait, the more pain and infection will be endured. I can't say confronting lying will "feel" good. In fact, the moments may feel like they're worse for dealing with it instead of turning a blind eye to it. But facilitating something that is false only breads emptiness, hurt, and separation.

(Side Note: if you are trying to justify letting your spouse continue in their lie, that is a huge red flag that something has to be dealt with.)

3. Walk in forgiveness. Forgiveness is the response to other's faults in proportion to how Christ responds to us. Forgiveness is not the same as trust or restoration. Forgiveness is the road that leads to trust and restoration.
4. Create expectations. Draw the line on lying. I'm not talking about ultimatums. I'm talking about developing a marriage that doesn't tolerate lying on ANY level. Healthy expectations set the bedrock of trust that will enable to see your spouse and marriage restored.
5. Celebrate progress. The lying has done enough breaking down of your spouse. Build up and encourage your him/her. You can't expect perfection but, with healthy and attainable expectations, you can celebrate steps forward through the process. Be a coach instead of a drill sergeant.

Our beginning scripture says it all: Having lips that speak truth will have an enduring effect upon your marriage.

Pursue truth together. Embrace truth as one. And, together, stand in truth and watch God do amazing things in you and through you.

- 15 -

"Permission Granted"
4 Reasons Why Unity in Your Marriage is Better than Permission

Permission is a funny thing. Permission, defined, is authorization or consent. Sadly enough, this is how a lot of marriages work. The reason why marriages work that way, is there is a misunderstanding of unity and Lordship. One of my favorite scriptures comes out of Acts 17:28 (ESV), "in him (Jesus) we live and move and have our being." It's through Jesus' provision and authority that we live our lives as well as our marriages.

This is where we screw it up. This is where we like to take authority that belongs to him, and exercise that over our spouse. Instead of working with our spouse, we want to lord over her spouse. It rips apart our oneness, and places us in the seat of a dictator. We make our spouse seek permission to spend money, to travel, to spend free time, or anything that they desire to do. The "permission thing" might seem healthy to you, but it's caging up your spouse and making them live in concern and or fear of you and your opinion. Fear has nothing to do with love. In fact fear wants to drive out love.

I want the two of you to stop asking for permission. I want the two of you to get the mindset out that you would need permission from your spouse to do anything. It doesn't mean we go and do everything that we

---

desire to do regardless of how our spouse feels. Means we communicate out of a desire to get a unified heart.

When I ask Anne about spending money, hanging out with friends, or to simply go out to a store, it's not about permission.

It's about unity.

I don't need my wife's permission for anything. I do want her unity. When I look in Psalms 133 (NLT), spells out 4 blessings that come from unity.

1. **Psalm 133 (NLT) says unity is "wonderful and pleasant."** What a great description for the atmosphere you bring to your home in marriage. I don't know if you've ever walked into a very awkward home or place, but if you have you want to leave it immediately. Homes with atmospheres where you must have "permission" is everything but "wonderful and pleasant." It's constructive, painful, and awkward. A unified heart between a husband and wife creates an atmosphere where the marriage can grow and where children can be raised because it is "wonderful and pleasant." Needing permission stinks up the room. Unity clears it up.

2. **Unity makes your marriage "precious" (verse 2).** This speaks of value. The greater unity you foster the more value you bring to your marriage and your spouse. Working in unity will bring value to your parenting. Your kids will see the family as valued. Is unity easy? Absolutely not. But the hard work and focus of unity continues to shape your marriage to make it precious and of extreme value. You want to show your spouse how valuable they are? Show that you want to walk in unity with him/her. Want to lose value, remove freedom and demand permission.

3. **Next, it says that unity is "refreshing."** There is enough of this world that wants to suck the life, joy, and love out of your life. When you come home, you should experience refreshing. Having to seek permission steals the joy from marriage away. Constantly having to ask for authorization, rips away the freedom Jesus desires

you to have. Fostering a unified hard between the two of you gives a place of refreshing. Conflict is not avoided, struggles are not bottled up, and issues I've never ignored because the two of you choose to walk in unity. **Please note this:** unity does it mean there's never a disagreement. It just means you choose to walk in unity regardless of opinion.

4. **Lastly, Psalms 133 (NLT) says where there is unity God "commands His blessing."** I think one of the biggest reasons here is because we've left the Lordship up to Jesus. We leave the "permission" thing up to him. We allow Jesus to have the authority. And when we walk in unity with each other and with Jesus, his blessing continues to rest upon our lives. This helps remove worry and exciting from marriage. When we go through rough patches and storms, when the season of life is treating us to well, we don't have to wring our hands in a worry. We know that the command and blessing of God will be upon us cause we're choosing to walk through it together in unity.

Unity thing works in every aspect. Even if your spouse is broken trust with you, The accountability he/she needs nothing to do with them asking for "permission." Has everything to do with communication for the sake of "unity."

If you been exercising Lordship over your spouse, today is the day to relinquish that to Jesus. Today is the day to ask for forgiveness from your spouse. Today is a new day for you to walk in unity in to see amazing results of God's blessings on your marriage.

- 16 -

"Eviction Notices"
8 Mindsets to Evict from
Your Marriage

For as he thinks within himself, so he is. Proverbs 23:7 (NASB)

I can't say that I've ever been given an eviction notice. But I assume it's not a good thing to get one. In my lifetime, I've had my power shut off before. I've even had collections call. But to get an eviction notice, that's something I do not desire to experience. It was about a year ago that our staff helped an individual who was being evicted. The experience of seeing everything the person owned thrown on the lawn was surreal to say the least. But to deal with the people whose family member was being evicted was quite the learning experience. This man went to bed in his "home" and woke up to not having a home.

Eviction notices. The notification telling someone who they are being expelled or kicked out from the place they called home. This is where Proverbs 23:7 (NASB) comes in.

"For as he thinks within himself, so he is."

The mind is a powerful thing. And carrying unhealthy mindsets in your marriage can cause your marriage to struggle far more than it needs to. There enough challenges in this world for your marriage and your mind shouldn't be the place where they start or are fed. When we conceive an unhealthy mindset about our marriage and/or about our spouse, we will ultimately live it out. It won't stay in the mind. Whatever it is you are entertaining in your thought life, you are inviting into the rest of your life. So today I'm challenging you to serve eviction notices to things that have been living in your mind.

7 Mindsets you need to evict:

1. **Assumption.** The old adage says, "When you assume you make a _____ out of U & ME" and it's just as true in our marriage. Fear drives assumption. It's the result of darkness in your relationship. When you don't know what has happened and/or what is going on (even in the little things), your mind is going to wander and indulge in wrong thinking. When you have communication breakdowns, assumption is the natural result and it will toy with your mind. How many times have you had a shift in your mood because assumption has filled your thoughts and changed your emotions? How many times do you find yourself mad, hurt, frustrated with your spouse AND you don't even know why? It's assumption.

Side note: If you are keeping ANYTHING from your spouse, don't complain about your spouse assuming things. Again, assumption is the natural result of invited darkness/mystery.

2. **Jealousy.** This is a negative mindset rooted in low self-esteem and fear. Spouses are more likely to be jealous when he/she doesn't believe he/she is lovable or that they are not worthy of being loved. People like this live in constant fear that their spouse will, first, see others more attractive and, second, take actions based upon those feelings. Jealousy rapes your mind. I know that's a strong word but it's the only way to project that damage it does. It will rob the individual experiencing it of value while ripping the trust from the marriage.

3. **Suspicion.** (Anne encouraged me to separate this from jealousy.) Many times, this isn't based on anything a spouse may or may

MOSAIC MARRIAGE | 63

not have done. It might not be about what he/she actually did or is presently doing. It may not be about what a spouse will ever do, Suspicion lives off of the "what could be" mindsets. Suspicion is demanding and unreasonable because the spouse doesn't have to do anything wrong. The fear is that they are losing that person and they have to do something to hold onto them, to test them and to make them understand that they are needed. If not dealt with, suspicion knows no reason and can be very detrimental to a relationship.

4. **Visual Pornography.** NOTE: This is not just a male issue. Both men and women can be visually stimulated. The goal of pornography is to skew the authentic with fantasy. Visual pornography is a huge stumbling block for couples and causes tremendous sexual issues. Two of my biggest reasons is it causes an unhealthy view of the female body as well as an unhealthy sexual expectations. Top it off with the addictive nature of porn devised to make you dependent upon it, you then have a monster that isn't worth the amount of space it will take up in your thoughts.

5. **Emotional Pornography.** I guess I could have lumped both kinds together, but like jealousy and suspicion, this second type of porn needed to be separate. Again, the goal of pornography is to skew the authentic with fantasy. Emotional porn may not fill you mind with naked people, but it will fill your imaginations with the skewed reality of where your marriage is at. Like it's counterpart, unhealthy scenarios of what your partner is/isn't doing, what you do/don't deserve, what you are/aren't experiencing fill your thoughts and develops unrealistic expectations that probably can never be met. Like a thirsty man crawling through the desert after a mirage, emotional porn has you crawling toward an illusion that will leave you constantly in want.

6. **Unforgiveness.** I can't bring this up enough. Unforgiveness is the best way to define what having "skeletons in the closet" means. Some of you are holding onto the bones of previous fights and issues that have long since died. But you still keep the remnants around. Maybe it's because of the hurt. Most the time it's for ammo

to use just in case a fight starts. Nevertheless, the bones/remains of past issues will haunt your mind unless they are released to be buried in time.

7. **Negativity.** Living life in a pessimistic state is miserable. Some people place themselves there because he/she feels they don't deserve anything good. It's like some sort of way of living out punishment. Others refuse to be positive because they've never known that growing up. They'll call it being the "realist" in the marriage. I'm, by nature, a dreamer so I recognize the need for a realist (Anne) in my life. She dreams with me but knows, at some point, the rubber must hit the road. Spouses who rent out space in their heads to the negative are miserable people. Stop giving yourself permission to be negative by saying you're a realist. That negativity in your mind is sucking the fun out of your life.

8. **Envy.** Why do we look at others and fixate on what they have and what we do not? We see others, compare our marriages, material possessions, and lifestyles and use them as ideals to chase. In our minds, we conjure up so much frustration with ourselves AND our spouse because what we don't have what others do. We then project that mindset onto our spouse and make them feel miserable because what they offer and who they are is never going to be enough.

I don't know what your mind is consumed with, but it's time to hand out eviction notices. It's time to identify the infectious crap that wants to cloud your minds and destroy your judgement. Remember, "For as he thinks within himself, so he is." Whatever it is you are entertaining in your thought life, you are inviting into the rest of your life. If you're struggling with your thought life, would you take a moment to confess it? It may sound crazy, but scripture says, "Confess your sins to each other and pray for each other so that you may be healed." James 5:16 (ESV)

We confess vertically to Jesus that we may be forgiven. We confess horizontally to someone (namely our spouse) that we can find healing.

Sit with your spouse, and pray. Take time to confess to the Lord what you're struggling with. He already knows what you're dealing with. He's faithful and just to forgive. Then talk with your spouse. Let him/her help you as you both move forward with minds that give no room for ANYTHING that has no right to take up space in your mind.

Guard your marriage by guarding your minds.

- 17 -

"Static-Filled Marriage"
2 Adjustments to Help
Tune-In Your Marriage

From the get-go, I'll say this: A well-defined picture of marriage is a life-long dedication to making personal and marital adjustments.

I remember the day my parents got a new TV and gave me the old one from the living room. As a kid, I hit the jackpot. Now you need to get out of you mind anything HD or plasma/flat screen. This is old-school. Nothing digital. It was a TV that had, what we called STATIC. Static was simply the disturbance in the picture and sound of what we were trying to enjoy.

And because of static, our TVs needed constant "tuning." From adjusting the "rabbit ears" to the dial around the channel knob (I've got a contingent of younger readers right now who have no idea what I'm talking about). In fact, around 8:00, a channel would shut down and turn to a pay-per-view for the Red Wings. What I did, with much finagling and attaching of wire hangers, I would get some semblance of a black and white picture mixed with the radio broadcast to enjoy 80's Red Wing hockey.

Static was a part of TV when I was growing up. This is what we had to endure back in the 80's and beyond (I'm only 40). Enjoying television in my room was an experience of constant small adjustment to get the best picture. Sometimes the modifications depended upon the channel.

Sometimes they depended upon the time of day. Nevertheless, it was worth it when you got to see the image you were looking for.

Honestly, it's such a beautiful metaphor for how marriage works.

God made man in His image. And I believe that the image of God is so complex that His likeness couldn't be contained to one person. The beauty of God is scene in marriage; man and woman coming together and showing a tremendous high-def picture of the likeness of God. But it's a picture that takes a lifetime of adjustments to work on THAT image to display.

And because we are human, we live a life of making constant adjustments in our personal lives knowing that we need to grow. Maturity is always needed. We tend to have grace for ourselves because we know we are definitely not a finished product.

So why can't we see our marriage in the same way? We have grace for ourselves but expect perfection for our spouse. Maybe you don't expect perfection, but perhaps our expectations are so high for our spouses that we've already set them up for failure. Perhaps if we see our spouses with the same amount of grace we give ourselves, we can see the life of our marriage as a journey of constant "tuning." I'm talking about **small adjustments** that will give the best picture of what marriage can look like. Sometimes the modifications depended upon the goal you are striving for. Sometimes the "tuning" will depend upon the season of life. Nevertheless, it will be worth it when you got to see the image you are looking for.

"Fix your thoughts on what is true, and honorable, and right, and pure, and lovely, and admirable. Think about things that are excellent and worthy of praise. Keep **putting into practice** all you learned and received from me—everything you heard from me and saw me doing. Then the God of peace will be with you." Philippians 4:8-9 (NLT)

What are some simple adjustments to help deal with marital static?

1. **Confront your mind with truth.** Our minds can get consumed with crap that may or may not be true. Our minds can get consumed with current situations and, on top of that, muddied with assumptions. Philippians 4 (NLT), Paul tells the local church how to properly fix your mind. When you are pondering on issues that are real and those that are assumption, fix your mind upon that which is true, honorable, right, pure, lovely, and admirable. Confront mindsets (assumptions, unrealistic expectations, bitterness, hurt) with the truth of God's Word. Fix your mind to it.

Wrapping your mind around what God says about your life helps bring definition to your situation. God's word confronts your thoughts with truth. It will take the scrambled picture of your marriage and bring order and color back into it.

Get a **view** of how God **looks** at you.
Get a **grasp** of how God **responds** to you.
Get a **grip** on how God **holds** you.
Get a **vision** of his **ridiculous** love for you.

I believe the more biblically literate your marriage is, the more growth you'll experience. Why? Because the more revelation of His image, the more you'll want to reflect (tune in) your life AND your marriage. This leads me to #2...

2. **Put truth into practice.** Don't leave God's word on the pages of your bible; live them out personally and relationally. Once you tune into how God SEES and RESPONDS to you, it empowers you to respond to your spouse. I mean, how can I receive the undeserved favor of God and not show the same amount of grace for my spouse?

What I love about Paul's words, "put this into practice" is that he doesn't give us an ending point. In other words, we don't stop "practicing." We don't stop tuning, adjusting, working, forgiving, loving, etc. It's the beauty of marriage. Work and longevity create the most beautiful high-def masterpiece. A well-defined picture of marriage is a life-long dedication to making personal and marital adjustments.

Don't get satisfied with the picture you have now because it will change. You will grow older. Seasons of life change. Atmospheres of life change. Life is about subtle changes and adjustments. In fact, I've heard it said that life is 20% of what happens to us and 80% of how we respond. Remember, static is simply the disturbance in the picture and sound of what we were trying to enjoy. Life will give you enough static to deal with. But you can respond to the static by simply...
...confronting your mindset with truth...
...and putting truth into practice.

"Fix your thoughts on what is true, and honorable, and right, and pure, and lovely, and admirable. Think about things that are excellent and worthy of praise. Keep **putting into practice** all you learned and received from me—everything you heard from me and saw me doing. Then the God of peace will be with you." Philippians 4:8-9 (NLT)

- 18 -

"Weekly Marriage Checklist"
8 Things EVERY Marriage Should
Be Doing On a Weekly Basis

Today I wanted to get into an incredibly practical marriage blog.

My wife and I are list makers. Even though we do our lists differently, it gives us both a sense of accomplishment to check them off. I use my phone. She's old school with pencil and paper. But nevertheless, we want to look over our days and week and feel we got done what needs to get done.

So today, I wanted to give you a simple checklist to help with some items, I believe, should be on your weekly radar.

Every week, I believe EVERY couple should have...

1. A Weekly Overview.
Anne and I have a standing appointment every Sunday night where we talk through our week. It's a simple touch to keep our communication and expectations on an appropriate level. We talk through our personal schedules. We talk though family schedules. It's here were we decide when dates, family connection, and downtime is needed. It's amazing how this little AND SIMPLE action can clear up what to expect and keep our communication healthy.

2. A Worship Point.

Being a part of a church community TOGETHER is a huge foundational piece of marriage. Being together to worship, serve, and engage in your church will help build relationships necessary for your personal growth as well as marital growth. On top of that, your involvement in your church community can be a tremendous blessing to others. See yourself as a part of a greater body. You are necessary to others and others are necessary to you.

3. A Date.

I think every couple can carve out of your week an hour or two. Do a meal, get some ice-cream, or go for a walk at a park. A date doesn't have to have much (if any) cost. Get out of your head that you need to do something extravagant (not that I'm against that) as a "date." I'm speaking to time for the two of you to have that relational connection you need.

4. Alone Time.

From hobbies to leisure time, having time to yourself is necessary. Don't get me wrong, I love time with Anne and she loves time with me. But it is healthy to have a few moments where there's a bit of separation. Anne and I don't watch all the same shows/movies. We don't enjoy all the same hobbies. That doesn't take away from our marriage. It adds to it.

5. A Place(s) of Generosity.

There is a true joy in being generous as a couple. When you give out of your time, talents, and treasure, you foster the heart of God (of which you were made in the image of). For almost two decades, Anne and I are faithful givers to our local church. We give to missions and benevolence. But we also look for opportunities to bless those in our community. Generosity will foster a depth of joy that so many people take for granted.

6. An Intimate Moment(s).

Sex and intimacy are not the same thing nor is Sex the source of intimacy. It should be seen as an expression of intimacy. Don't get me wrong, I believe that healthy marriages have a consistent sex-life. What the frequency looks like isn't up to you the individual. It's what has been agreed upon by both you and your spouse (prevents one libido from lording over the other). But remember: Intimacy doesn't always include sex. It is far deeper. It's that intimate connection where you selflessly serving your spouse's love language. Intimacy doesn't have to fade in your marriage, it just looks different over time. Find what your spouse's love language is and look to serve it without strings attached (expectations of reciprocation). When you connect the heart of your spouse, that is intimacy.

7. Laughter/Fun.
(This is a bit more than a scheduled event. It's more of an element that's needed.) Couples that schedule fun moments are far healthier on EVER level (mental, emotional, physical, and spiritual). Anne and I will watch clips on Youtube in the evenings. Sometimes we'll send them to each other over Facebook messenger. Maybe you two like games and/ or activities. It could be movies or books. Find what the other enjoys that fills your marriage with smiles.

8. Heavy Encouragement.
This should be a daily point instead of a weekly one. My rule I give couples all the time: Don't let anyone out-encourage you when it comes to your spouse. For too often, people only speak up when they see something wrong. Why do we build that culture in our marriages? Catch your spouse doing something right. From accomplishments to even just the simple effort to attempt something, find ways to fill your spouse full of encouragement.

Obviously, this list isn't exhaustive. There's probably some other things you can add to it specifically for your marriage. But, in my opinion, these are essentials that I don't think couples can do without.

Love Jesus passionately.
Love your spouse passionately.
Make both a heavy priority in your life.

- 19 -

"Needed Time:
A Time Starved Marriage"
4 Suggestions for Balancing
Quality Time

Yesterday we celebrated our anniversary. This occasion is a time of reflection. We spent the evening eating and shopping and reminiscing over the past decade and a half. There's no way Anne and I have arrived. But we've come a long way. We have gone through a lot of struggles. And if there's anything that I've struggled at in our marriage from the beginning it's with this issue of "time."

Anne married a "work-a-holic." She married someone who couldn't say "no" to people. My heart as a pastor is to help. So my excuse for not taking a day off or vacations for the first few years of marriage was my compassion for the people I pastored and the loyalty to the church I served. From one angle, it sounds admirable. The reality: there's nothing admirable about it. When sharing this testimony to people, I've heard, "well it's because you're such a good pastor." I cannot be a good pastor if I'm a rotten husband. I'll be blunt about it,

Starving your spouse for their "needed time" is abusive.

It got worse. I was a fan of playing "wallyball" (simply said, it's volleyball played using the walls of a racquetball court). I had some of my friends that would play it on a weekly basis. On top of that, I was playing softball. I felt needed my time with the guys. My long days at work, in my mind, afforded me the right to do what I wanted in the evenings. After all, I work hard. In all of this, I still came home to a time-starved wife. Her words made me feel guilty and I covered up the guilt with arguments and attitudes. She had "needed time" too but was abandoned to deal with it on her own. I'll say it again...

Starving your spouse for their "needed time" is abusive.

Was my job/ministry so important that she needed to take a back seat to it all? What was the worth of being able to pay the mortgage on a home if my home-life was falling apart from neglect? I forgot that my wife is my first ministry. Outside of Christ, she is priority for my time and energy. But I wasn't getting that into my thick skull. I was so out of balance. I used the excuse of "quality time together" for the time we spent with my or her parents. We didn't date. Unless we were in bed, we didn't spend time alone. We were both starving for "needed time."

In his letter to the Ephesians, Paul cautioned the church, "Be very careful, then, how you live – not as unwise but as wise, making the most of every opportunity, because the days are evil" (Ephesians 5:15-16 NIV). Living "wise" involves using our time carefully. In fact, the word "wise" in the Greek means, "forming the best plans and using the best means for their execution." As believers, we are supposed to look at our time and form a strategy so that our time spent is of the utmost quality.

"Needed time" is a phrase that means "appropriate and QUALITY time that feeds a healthy balanced life."

"Needed time" for you and your spouse looks like...

Quality time with God - I learned a quote from a preacher years ago. "You can't draw out of a dry well." As a preacher, it's hard for me to pour into someone's life if nothing has been poured into me. My relationship is only healthy in my marriage because it is the outpouring of my relationship with Jesus. I learn to love from Christ. I learn to forgive through Him. I know how to serve from reading about how He served humanity. It is very hard to direct you to do anything healthy in your marriage without starting with the one who transformed my life and my marriage: Jesus Christ.

Quality time together - What does quality time look to your spouse? Have you asked him/her? Do you already know the answer? Do you refuse to ask/inquire because it's not your view of what quality time looks like? You two need time together that feeds each other's need so that your relationship can grow while meeting each other's needs. He may want to work on a project with you. She may want to be intimate. Quit fighting about who is getting he better end of the deal. Learn to serve each other and listen to a scripture I quote a lot to couples. Philippians 2:4 (ESV) says "Let each of you look not only to his own interests, but also to the interests of others." Anne and I didn't start off that way. We've had to learn to not be selfish with our time together. We have known what the other likes. And we have learned that pleasure doesn't some from receiving but giving.

Time apart - You probably didn't see this one coming. I encourage couples to make sure that there is appropriate time apart. Some of your needs are going to be met by people other than your spouse. What I mean by that is this: Sometimes husbands need to be with the guys...sometimes wives need to go out with the ladies. But this is done in balance. If your time with others dwarfs your time with your spouse, you have life out of balance. Anne and I have both look at the other and said, "you need to go have time with your friends!" There are times she needs another woman to talk to. I need to bat with other guys. It's a definite need that's there and your spouse will really appreciate it when you see the need in their life. It speaks of your ability to see their needs. But you will never have guilt free time apart if you are not giving QUALITY time with your spouse (notice I used QUALITY again).

**I do want to caution your time apart. Every couple I take through premarital counseling gets a warning about spending too much time with unmarried friends. I have a lot of unmarried friends. But I have to be careful, not necessarily about the amount of time, but the activities we do. Some couples have, or are, living out fantasies of singleness apart from their spouses. Be cautious of where you go and what you do as to not add temptation or suspicion in your marriage.

Time alone - Sometimes you need to be alone. Even Jesus went off to a solitary place (Mark 1:35 ESV). If the only time you are alone is in the bathroom, then you need personal break. If your wife has been around kids all day...for Pete's sake, come home, get the kids, and give her time alone. (Side note: it's not babysitting your kids...it's called being a parent.) Every one of us needs a break from humans to unwind and be refreshed. Anne and I both run on our own to clear our minds. I use it as time to pray and decompress. Look for ways to give your spouse the "alone" time they need. Of all of the things I've done for Anne that she adores, giving her time alone is at the top of her list...especially in the summer when the kids are out of school.

Keep watch over the time in your marriage. Don't abuse your spouse by starving them for the "needed time" in their life.

- 20 -

"What my parents didn't teach me about marriage"
3 Lessons I Gleaned From My Parents

I say it unashamedly: My parents are amazing.

Nope...you won't need to wait for the "other" shoe to drop. There is no "but" as if I was going to use the blog-osphere to blast Hal and Linda (my parents) and my criticism of their job at raising me and my sister.

Please don't take any of the following paragraphs as a guilt trip to those who have struggled or have made mistakes. I do not elevate anyone above Christ. But I do obey scripture to "give honor to whom honor is due."

But I found myself in a mode a few weeks ago. I had been doing some pre-marital counseling, received phone calls from other pastors about marriage issues, and had been reading some marriage blogs. As I read the blogs and thought though my phone calls, I realized something about some of the unhealthy marital situations I was a privy to:

I didn't see many of those issues growing up.

Don't get me wrong. Hal and Linda Barringer have their issues. How do I know that? I have issues and I'm told I have a lot of them (especially my father) in me. So they are not perfect in the least.

But...it began with a small list. And with that small list, I want to pour out in a series of blogs the things my parents didn't teach me.

First, what didn't my parents teach me? They didn't teach me that the children were priority over the marriage.

I knew dad loved mom. I knew mom loved dad. I knew that when the nest was empty, what I had seen before me would last because their marriage didn't stop because of 3 children born. Even when tragedy hit our home and my younger brother went to be with Jesus, what I saw before me was a strong marriage (not perfect) founded in a faith in One who has the strength, mercy, grace, and peace to get our family through ANYTHING! They will forever be living testimonies of that.

Why are so many marriages failing in the mid-years of life? There are numbers of things I could list. At the top of the list, there are those that put their marriage on hold because of children. Hal and Linda did not. They didn't teach me that. In fact they taught me the contrary.

In my years of being at home, not once if I expressed I needed them, did my parents ever fail at stepping up. We were not spoiled (even though I think my little sister was more spoiled than me...but that's an older brother speaking). There wasn't a single football game that was parentless. Every major event in my life, was always guarded in their prayers, involvement, and wisdom. I know they have regrets...but who amongst us can't look back with 20/20 and want to change things to make things better?

What Rachael and I viewed was strong. They would hang out with friends. They served together in ministry. They prayed together. They laughed together. To the chagrin of me and Rach, they kissed and hugged in front of us (which still disturbs me).

But know this: I, as a child/teen, NEEDED them to place their marriage as priority. I need to see a father defend his wife. I needed a parent structure that had a unified front. For my life as child and teen, I need to view two people who stuck together, through the power of Christ, traverse through life-events that have the power to cripple marriages. I didn't need a best friend(s). I needed parents. School and church provided me with the friendships to fill those needs. I needed mom to love dad and dad to love mom. I needed my parents, together, put their marriage as a priority. Because of that, I benefited with the structure and example I needed to know what a healthy Christ-centered marriage looks like. And for that, I am eternally grateful.

Mom and dad, you didn't teach me that your marriage was secondary to anybody or anything. When I think of you, I think of 1 Corinthians 11:1 (NIV): Follow my example, as I follow the example of Christ.

That's what I've done. I've followed you. Like you, I've got some regrets with my 20/20 hindsight (hey, we're human). But me, Anne, and my children are very grateful that they have you to follow.

Secondly, what didn't my parents teach me? They didn't teach me to operate separate from my spouse. They showed a unified front.

When I think of the definition of "oneness", I think of my parents. As stated in earlier, I don't think they're perfect in the least bit, but I'm grateful for them NOT teaching me certain things.

One of things they NEVER taught me was "disunity."

When I saw them make decisions, I heard discussions. They both gave input. Sometimes they asked us kids what we thought (even thought our opinions probably had no bearing on a decision). But nevertheless, we (Rach and I) felt a part of things. When dad and mom made the decision to go into ministry, tons of changes were coming to our lives. They told me of the news together.

To take this unity thing further, never once did I feel they vied for the position of "favorite parent." I never heard language or saw actions in which one was trying to be the "nice parent" and the other would be the "disciplinarian." It wasn't about "wait till _____ gets home." When it came to encouragement AND discipline, both parents shared the roles and walked in unity with those roles. If they disagreed on how the other one parented (which probably happened as I know it happens to me and Anne), I, as their child, never saw it and assumed it happened out of earshot of us kids.

Let's go another step deeper: When dad and mom had disagreements, we (Rach and I) were not pawns in the midst of conflict. Our heads were not filled with parents wanting us to take sides. We were not in the awkward position of hearing information that kids should hear. Our young minds didn't go through the agonizing conflict that so many parents put their kids through pressuring them to "side with mom/dad". We were spared from being a part of the conflict. They kept it between them.

One of my favorite scriptures to quote when talking marriage is Psalm 133 (ESV). For where there is unity, "...there the Lord commands His blessing."

There wasn't perfection in our home. There wasn't a world with rose-colored glasses (idealism). We lived modestly. We lived real. There was laughter and tears; excitement and disappointment. It was just a real home, with real issues, but approached by a marriage in a unified manner.

And for that reason, I believe the blessing of God was on us.

For that reason, I thank you mom and dad for being "one".

Lastly, what didn't my parents teach me? They didn't teach me to withhold encouragement.

I stand by a statement I said to our congregation at Kfirst on March 23rd, 2013:

"If you are NOT an encourager, you will NEVER become the spouse/ parent God wants you to be."

That message was a crossroads for me as a believer and pastor. I remember the season of ministry I was in. It was astounding the amount of people (including pastors) that were calling me just discouraged. They were broken and bruised. These people were either beat up by discouragement or starved by the lack of encouragement.

What does that have to do with what I learned from my parents and or marriage? Well, first of all, they were married. Secondly, they are pastors. I have seen them discouraged in life and ministry. Yet of all of the things they didn't teach me, they didn't teach me to allow their circumstances to make them serve encouragement sparingly.
I don't think of a single time in my life where I didn't see them encourage each other, their children, or the congregation they served. I can't even recall moments in my life as a child/teen/adult where they were not the first to step up as an encourager in my life. Believe me, they've had every excuse to not be encouraging. I've seen people treat them terribly. As a pastor's kid, I've watched discouraging moments happen to them. People have taken advantage of their kindness. Others have turned their back on them. Circumstances have come and gone that would've depleted anyone of joy...yet, no excuses were given and words of edification were always in great supply.

Now, I recognize that many people (possibly you the reader) never had that growing up and/or have it now as an adult. As stated in my first blog of this series, they're not perfect. But their example has shown me this:

No matter if you had someone to encourage you in your past or not... No matter what you are dealing with right now...

No matter if there's no one in your corner right now...
...you can and should be an encourager.

Proverbs 11:25 (NIV) "those who refresh others will themselves be refreshed."

The cycle of discouragement must stop here and NOW. You may have an excuse to not encourage. We all do. I know my parents did and probably still do. Life is hard. Sometimes life just plain sucks. But there's something powerful about the issue of encouragement: when we launch out to refresh others, we get refreshed. I don't believe the refreshing comes from others. I believe it comes from the Lord. If you are depending upon your spouse (or anyone for that matter) to be the one to "fresh" you, it is clear that your life is centered upon deriving meaning, purpose, and joy from limited finite sources. In Christ we find life. And it's from Him we get refreshed.

Stop waiting for others to refresh and replenish you. Don't wait for your spouse to be the one to take the first step. Christ didn't wait till we were ready to receive him to give hope to our discouraging circumstances. He gave.

And because he gave...we too can give.

Keep encouraging. Keep refreshing and let Christ help you become the spouse you need to be.

- 21 -

"The Little Things"

If you watch enough TV, movies or even YouTube, you get a feeling that you are set up for romantic disaster. There are so many things to watch that make us feel romantically inadequate.

If you watch an episode of some dating show like "The Bachelor", you'll see people romancing each other with, what seems to be, no budgetary and/or resource (restaurants, settings, transportation, etc) restrictions. You'll watch movies (probably romantic comedies) where the romantic actions are done with immense proportions that almost makes you feel like you don't love your spouse because you've never did something on that scale.

We can get so wrapped up in a cultural philosophy called: Bigger is better. But I submit to you this: I like planning big things. I like making memorable moments. But (to use a cliché) it's the little things that count.

We look at all of those shows/movies thinking...
...ONE BIG event is going to propel us into marital health.
...ONE BIG moment will save our marriage.
...ONE BIG date/weekend will heal us.

It's like saying, "one trip to the doctor will make it all better." Seeing your family physician is good for you. It's definitely needed. But what creates health is every day action steps that follow the visit (fluids, eating properly, medicine, etc). The "ONE BIG" date or moment isn't bad for your marriage. But like the doctor visit, it's the little EVERY DAY things/actions/moments that follow the moment that really matter.

Proverbs 14:15 (NIV) The simple believes everything, but the prudent gives thought to his steps.

Can I get you to be prudent with your steps and think smaller? Can we get past "ONE BIG thinking" and into the wisdom of "little thing thinking"? Thinking like...

- The first few minutes your with your spouse in the morning will set the pace for the entire day.
- How you leave each other for the day can decide how anxious he/she will be to see you again.
- How you greet each other when you reunite for the evening speaks volumes.
- "Please" and "thank you" help your spouse not to feel taken for granted.
- Reaching your arm around your spouse in bed to pray for him/her speak volumes as well as depths of spiritual commitment.

But why stop there? Start getting practical and creative with "little things"...

- Send/give small thoughts or gestures (notes/texts/messages). If your spouse travels, leave messages in his/her luggage.
- Authentic affection (NOT laced with sexual expectations) will foster deeper intimacy.
- Spontaneous gestures of serving/selfless activity (clean/cook/fix).
- Care for what he/she cares about.
- If you are a parent, give your spouse some relief from the kids. As the old saying goes, "silence is golden."
- Use little touches to his/her love languages (acts of service, gifts, quality time, words of affirmation, physical touch).

It doesn't take much. Most of this stuff you won't see on "The Bachelor". But what the shows and movies won't tell you, it's the little things that keeps a marriage healthy and fun.

Be prudent and give careful thoughts to your steps to doing some "little things" every day with/for your spouse.

What ideas do you have? What little things do you do?

- 22 -

"Ten Things I Hate About My Spouse"

If you were to ask your friends/family/coworkers to make a "TOP TEN" list for you, what type of list would they make? Would it be, "Ten Things I Hate About My Spouse"? Or would it be "Ten Things I Love About My Spouse"?

I almost borrowed the title of the 1999 teen romance film, "Then Things I Hate About You." But I didn't want to make you think we were just turning this blog into a movie review for lame movies from our past.

Between recent blog-posts and a pre-marital counseling appointment, one theme has been constantly staring at me in the face: Marriage Edification. Of my marriage blogger friends, this week must have highlighted a theme that either they organized (without telling me) OR the Holy Spirit was trying to speak something specific into marriages.

Even this morning, I went through my early morning routine of waking up and immediately checking my twitter feed. There were more edification blogs. I did a quick count of 3 edification blogs in 12 hours that, specifically, was wives edifying their husbands. With titles like: "Why I love my husband", "Reasons I love my husband", and "11

Reasons I love my sexy husband", it seems everyone is on a similar page. These wives were sharing things like:

- He laughs with me.
- He flirts with me in front of the kids
- He lets me wear his sweatshirts
- I trust him with my heart
- (my personal favorite) When I asked him to get rid of the "whitey-tighties," he did.

Do you have a "Top Ten"? Can you come up with 10?
The question came: Have we stopped edifying our spouse? How do I speak about my spouse?

A simple definition of edify is to build up. One dictionary says to verbalize especially so as to encourage intellectual, moral, or spiritual improvement.
Maybe we can make it simpler: To uplift.

When we were courting our spouse, we were filled with words that caught the ear of the one we were in love with. There were phrases spoken that unashamedly expressed feelings and sensations. Even to friend and family around you, there was no mistake how you felt. Some of those words came out in a written letter. Other times it was over the phone. No matter the method, those days were times where your words could not be contained by silence. Your date/fiancé knew exactly what you felt and why you felt that way.

Does he/she still feel edified?

Now a days, we don't verbalize anything but criticism to our spouse. They hear nothing but shortcomings and put downs. Even worse, maybe all he/she gets from you is silence.

What about the people you talk/Facebook/email to? What do they hear you say about your spouse? Is it words like, "can you believe HE did this?" and "you'll never guess what SHE expected me to do."

I'll ask you the initial question we asked earlier in the blog: If you were to ask your friends/family/coworkers to make a "TOP TEN" list for you, what type of list would they make? Would it be, "Ten Things I Hate About My Spouse"? Or would it be "Ten Things I Love About My Spouse"?

Where would their information come from?

- Your conversations with them
- The way you talk to your spouse in public
- Your body language when your spouse walks into the room
- The way you talk to your spouse in front of the kids

By our words and actions, would they have a stronger case for the "hate" list over the "love" list?

Hebrews 3:13 is what jumps out to me. "But encourage one another daily, as long as it is called Today, so that none of you may be hardened by sin's deceitfulness."
Do you hear the warning? Encourage DAILY. If you don't, the results are painful. Your marriage will be hardened. Unfeeling. Deceived. I understand the context of the passage was speaking, generally, to all of God's people. I think it would be VERY appropriate to carry that principle into our marriage. Choosing to not edify your spouse is asking for a hardened and callused marriage.

You cannot assume your spouse knows how you feel! They need to hear it. They need to see it. Then take it a step further: edify your spouse to the people around you. It will accomplish four things:

1. Pleases the heart of God.
2. Rekindles your passion by uplifting the one you have become one with.
3. It will get back to your spouse and, thus, rekindle their passion.
4. Leaves no room for the enemy to fill the need for edification by anyone else.

Take some time to make a "top ten" list. Share it over dinner. Share it on a date (unless you're in a theater then wait till after). Even better, share it in bed. It's great pillow talk.

- 23 -

"Gold and White"
6 things the "Tumblr Dress"
taught me about marriage

I'm sitting watching a show with my daughter and during a commercial, I happened to look down at my twitter feed.

Big mistake. The world was crazy with over the color of a dress. This web-phenom started with a Tumblr post. A lady posted a picture of a two-toned dress with the caption, "Guys please help me-is this dress white and gold, or blue and black? Me and my friends can't agree and we are freaking...out." (edited out the f-bomb)

Within hours, the image went viral and consumed social network. I was lost. Everybody was posting, tweeting, and retweeting. Before, long, I heard Anne call me from the other room asking me about it. It didn't take long, but after spending a few moments (that I will NEVER get back) I found out what the world was obsessed with this dress and the actually color it was (I still don't know).

And I don't really get the big deal. But I did learn something about marriage.

6 things the "Tumblr Dress" taught me about marriage.

1. **Some people just love to argue.** You see them on Facebook and Twitter. Some of you see them when you wake up in the morning. People think it's fun to get a rise out of others. I've counseled couples in which the one who loves to argue has not clue that their method of "fun" is what's driving their spouse away. If you are one of those people who love to intentionally engage in unnecessary conflict and you are married to someone who is NOT like you...I've got some advice for you: Stop trying to stir up arguments all the time. It's not cute and you're annoying the crap out of your spouse.

2. **You're not going to agree on everything.** Stop thinking you do. If you disagree on stuff, there's nothing wrong with your marriage. If you two agree on everything, then one of you is not necessary. You may just need to agree to disagree. Which leads me to #3...

3. **Arguments mean you are not compatible...AND THAT'S A GOOD THING.** Compatibility is a farce. So many people (and dating websites) are bent on this being the "end-all" of relationships. Compatibility attracts...and that's all it's limited to. But it doesn't make a marriage. In fact, the word "compatible" means, "Able to exist or occur together without conflict." The incompatibility of your lives gives room for the two of you to work, love, and grow together. Your marriage is WAY RICHER because you've married to somebody who is much DIFFERENT than YOU are.

4. **Perception is more reality than you think.** Sometimes we are so bent on changing our spouse's perception. I'm not saying that's a bad thing, but there's a small process to it. First, validate their perception. He/she sees something you do not. Instead of making them feel wrong/stupid/ignorant, let him/or her feel valued by understanding what they see. Second, clearly and calmly explain your understanding to the situation. Third, if needed, apologize. Even if your actions are misunderstood, your actions did lead to the misunderstanding (a little extra humility never hurt anyone). Lastly, let the response of your actions change the perception.

5. **Don't tell me you two have nothing to talk about.** There's always something to talk about. The world stopped to talk about a dress (which I think is gold and white). What's really happened is one or both of you have quit trying to talk. You'll push yourself at work, church, the story, etc. to engage with people. Your spouses deserves that effort and more.

6. **You don't have to be right all the time**. You like it. I know I enjoy being right. For a portion of my marriage, even if I was wrong, I could manipulate the conversation to make Anne feel responsible for the situation so that I could be right. It was wrong. It's still wrong. If you are bent on ALWAYS being right makes you less attractive and more of a jerk. So stop it.

In the midst of all of this, I find myself in Proverbs 18:15 (MSG). It says, "Wise men and women are always learning, always listening for fresh insights."

I'm a guy who's always trying to learn. I am looking for ways to grow. As silly as this whole dress thing is, there's so much we can learn from our human responses. And if we don't pursue opportunities to learn, we will pay for it personally as well as martially. To learn is to live. And in the words from one of my favorite movies, "Get busy living or get busy dying."

Now that the "Tumblr Dress" has had its 15 minutes of fame...this blog is officially outdated.

- 24 -

"My Marriage is Full of Crap"
5 ways to make fertilizer
for the future

From the get-go, let me say this: Storms don't discriminate. They're equal opportunity givers.

Like the word "crap" or not. Every one of us have that/a word we utilize to describe a moment that didn't suit us. It could encapsulate an entire event or the immediate feeling about the situation. We all have our "word." You may be more sanctified than me (most likely), but "Crap" seems to be the one I settled on years ago that seems to be a family fav. For those of you already offended by the word, you're probably wondering when the blog about the "looseness of words" is going to happen. But that's another blog for another time.

22 days from now, Anne and I will celebrate 17 years of marriage together. And after our 20 years of being "Dave and Anne" (dating and marriage), I can say, our marriage has been full of crap, or more descriptive, crappy situations. There have been moments of disappointment and displeasure. Frustrations and faults. We have annoyed each other and let each other down. We've seen embarrassment and hurt.

Yet here we stand. I don't say that out of any semblance of pride. I humbly recognize that which the Apostle Paul recognized, "I can do everything through Christ, who gives me strength." Philippians 4:13 (NLT)

Some of you see the "crap" that has happened and you feel alone. Even though in your head, you know others deal with it, but your experiences make you feel you're on a desert island...alone and stuck. Maybe you're like me and as you watch things transpire, you feel like a failure because you could've/should've prevented it from happening. It's frustrating but tough moments are a part of life you can't always forecast. But you can do one of two things:

1. Wallow in the crap. We can just sit/live in the frustration and disappointment. The filthiness and smell of failure can be your new identity. We can walk around reeking like it because we refuse to leave it behind.

or...

2. We can take the "crap" life throws at us and turn it into fertilizer. You and I can look at a "set-back" and use it as a "set-up" for something amazing to happen.

One of my favorite professors in college used to say, "You need to have 50/20 vision." The scripture he was referring to was a passage in Genesis spoken from the mouth of Joseph. You want to talk about "crap" happening to someone. He was betrayed by family. Sold into slavery. Lost a position of authority out of a false sex scandal. Jailed. Forgotten in obscurity.

Yet when all is said and done, he stands on the other side of a lifetime of letdowns with these words to the very family who tried to destroy him, "Don't you see, you planned evil against me but God used those same plans for my good." Genesis 50:20 (MSG)

The moments happen. Those unplanned and unforeseen moments that we never thought would happen to our marriage blindsided us. Nobody plans for disappointments. There's not a single one of us who walked the aisle of our weddings wishing that we could have frustration in our marriage.

But it happens. You are human. You married a human. Humans are messy. "Crap" is going to happen. But you have the choice: wallow in it or see it with 50/20 vision. See it from a place where God can use it to fertilize growth for the future.

Here's a few tips for you to get 50/20 vision of the "crap" that happens...

1. **Guard your responses.** The book of James tells us, "Understand this, my dear brothers and sisters: You must all be quick to listen, slow to speak, and slow to get angry." This is a 3-part message by itself. Don't be reactionary. Take time to ponder and process what is taking place. See past the surface into the deeper issues. Perhaps your spouse isn't trying to hurt you purposely, but he/she is acting out of her themselves. Take a moment to listen thoroughly, carefully choose healthy words, and calm your temperament.

2. **Be careful who you surround yourself with.** Psalm 1 warns us to be cautious to not surround ourselves with people who are NOT going to have a healthy, Godly mindset. But joyous living comes from surrounding yourself with the wisdom (Word) of God. When we do, the promise is we will be like a like "trees planted along the riverbank, bearing fruit each season. Their leaves never wither, and they prosper in all they do." I don't care if the person is your BFF, if the person is all about telling you what you want to hear and/or what they selfishly want for you, you need to separate yourself from them during this season. When the "crappy" moments of life hit, the wisdom (or lack thereof) you surround yourself with can make all the difference in the world.

3. **Be a bridge builder.** We're always waiting for others to make the first move. Some say, "Time heals everything." It's a lie. Time, by itself, heals nothing. The only way to resolve conflict is to face it. God expects you to take the first step. He expects you to be the peacemaker. You make the first move. It doesn't matter if you are the offended one or the offender. Always see it as your move. It's so important that God says it takes priority over worship. Matthew

5:23-24 (NLT) says, "So if you are presenting a sacrifice at the altar in the Temple and you suddenly remember that someone has something against you, leave your sacrifice there at the altar. Go and be reconciled to that person. Then come and offer your sacrifice to God."

4. **See what Christ sees.** Potential is recognizing the future possibility. It's unrealized power. This is the way Christ sees us. He sees His power working in us and what can be done/accomplished through Him if we will walk in obedience. NOTE: He doesn't wait for our actions to begin to see who we could be. He doesn't wait for our obedience to respond to us. Jesus reaches out when we don't. He offers a future without us even deserving it. Your spouse may look and act like a mess. But if you'll look in the mirror, you're not going to see any less in you. This is why we all need to see what Jesus sees. Always look past the surface and see the potential.

5. **Love based upon His love and not yours.** 1 Corinthians 13 (NLT) has been read at so many weddings. I've done it. I've heard it. We constantly read it from the place of how we are supposed to love. We really need to see it as a description of how God loves. Us humans carry such a surface level understanding of love. It's so dependent upon "what have you done for me lately." We fall "out" of love as fast as we fall "in" love. Paul tells a Corinthian church who is struggling with an understanding of love, sex, and community that THIS is what God's love looks like. It's not a circumstantial feeling. It's a daily decision. And if we are going to reflect Him, we need to daily decide to respond to the world around us, especially our spouse, with His love.

Crap happens to all of us. Storms don't discriminate. They're equal opportunity givers. But today you need to decide: Are you going to wallow in it? Or are you ready to turn it around to fertilize your future and launch your marriage towards health.

It time to move forward and see God do amazing things.

- 25 -

A "Yesterday Marriage"
5 ways to help your marriage
to not live off of re-runs

Of all of our differences, Anne and I don't really walk in agreement with the concept of re-runs. We both love shows and enjoy watching them together. But re-runs are a different story. I can only think of one show series in our entire marriage in which she'll entertain the re-runs. But other than that, she watches a show and moves on. I am her polar opposite. I thrive on re-runs. M*A*S*H, The West Wing, Taxi, and Whose Line are just a few I can't get enough of (not to mention I'll watch old football games...she totally doesn't get that). I love the nostalgia of it as well as the opportunity of passing great shows onto my kids. Cammi loves a few of them (Saved by the Bell, Leave it to Beaver). Ethan shot down most of them after 5 minutes of the first episode. (Macgyver, A-Team, Battlestar Galactica).

Re-runs take you back in time (without a flux capacitor). Even just hearing theme songs, you can picture yourself in another time and place. Things seemed much simpler...less complicated. They can even provide you with a sense of security. Unfortunately, instead of enjoying the reflective nature of nostalgia, we tend to make it a place to live.
This is a dangerous place for marriages. I call them "Yesterday Marriages." They are couples where someone (or both spouses) are living in the past. They have the inability to move forward because they

are living off of the re-runs of their marriage. You can't change your marriage living on re-runs.

5 ways to help your marriage to not live off re-runs:

1. **Drop your subscription to unhealthy storylines.** Anne and I are Hulu and Netflix people (this blog isn't sponsored by either). The reason we subscribe to them is they provide us with the entertainment we desire. Some of you are subscribed to attitudes that are unhealthy to your marriage. By "subscribe," I mean you know you are doing it but do nothing about it. Lack of action is an action in of itself. It means you are welcoming it. Bitterness, negativity, ingratitude, and the like are attitudes that are designed corrode any sibilance of joy in your marriage. They'll create storylines that are unnecessary. Drop your subscription to that storyline and move on.

2. **Know your ratings; check your emotions.** I'm an emotional guy and I believe that feelings are important. To have emotions proclaims our humanity. Yet, like anything in life, we are called to be stewards of our emotions. A few weeks ago, I challenged our congregation to do exactly what the Psalmist does in Psalms 42 (NLT): question your emotions. He questions his emotions 3 times. Why? We base truth by how we feel. I know this doesn't apply to you, but my emotions change daily. I can be (not all the time) irrational. If truth is how we feel, then truth shifts and changes based upon whether we had coffee, had sex with our spouse, or our NCAA bracket is going okay. Call your emotions into question and base truth upon who Christ is. We are to bring truth to our marriage rather than allowing feelings/circumstances to dictate truth to us.

3. **Shut off the drama**. We were meant to live in community/relationships. I believe God moves in community. But that which God uses, Satan perverts. People that crave drama love to create it and feed it. They're easy to identify. Look at

what they post on social media. Look at what they reference whenever they contact you to you. If they're poking at your past and/or asking about business that isn't theirs to know or be involved with, then they're trying to get you to entertain "re-runs." Get some boundaries with them. Draw some lines and shut off the drama. They're not propelling you towards health. They are an anchor to you moving forward.

4. **Cancel the series.** Anne and I have mourned the cancellation of certain series (Jericho is one that comes to mind). If you're entertaining unhealthy thoughts of the past, then it's time to stop subscribing to them. It's a choice. Don't tell me it's not. You may not be able to stop the thought from popping up in your head but you DO have a choice on how long that thought lingers. Lust, unforgiveness, comparing marriage, fantasies about having a different spouse are all networks that have not right being in your head feeding re-runs of what life "could have been." Shut them down. Cancel the series.

5. **New episodes cannot happen without new material.** You can't develop anything new if you don't do anything new. Marriages can't move on from re-runs if there's nothing new to work with. Memories are created with opportunities. Some of the reasons your marriage might be boring is, well, you are boring. Get out and do something. It doesn't have to cost anything. Anne and I enjoy taking walks (zero cost) and talking about our day (zero cost). We love sitting on our bed watching shows together ($7.99 a month). New material for new memories doesn't take much money if all, but it Take a drive. Get some ice cream. Be simple but creative. Your spouse would rather you fail trying than fail to try. Make time. Your spouse is worth it.

You can't change your world on re-runs. It's time to move forward. Most people are looking for the fresh start because, in their mind, it's the only place to start. Instead of thinking you need a new spouse for a new start, start with a new you for your present spouse.

Living on "re-runs" places a whole lot of trust in ourselves and in a fantasy world of "what could be." There is no promise in that. But people just cast their marriage aside with empty hope, praying that the next time through will be better. The problem is: you carry the same "re-run" issues into the next marriage. 2 Corinthians 5:17 (NLT) says "This means that anyone who belongs to Christ has become a new person. The old life is gone; a new life has begun!"

Instead of scrapping your marriage, scrap the old you and put on the new you in Christ. Instead of placing your trust in you, place your faith in Christ and live life from that place. What you will discover is the hope that we have in Christ moves our fixation off of us and our past, and places our focus upon who we are in him. You need a fresh start and a fresh place to work from? Become new in Christ and let him, not your re-runs be the foundation of a new future for your marriage.

Don't have a "yesterday marriage." Get out of the past and see the future you two have together in Christ.

- 26 -

"Not What I Was Expecting"
6 Ways to Develop Healthy
Marital Expectations

I sat with some great friends and enjoyed some frozen yogurt while sharing stories of early "moments" in marriage where we may not have been at our best. First, I'm glad to have relationships where Anne and I can get together with others and laugh (still laughing about the Spam story). Laughter is a medicine to your soul (Prov. 17:22 NLT). It's a necessity for a healthy emotional state. Secondly, it's such a necessity to have relational outlets for you two to go out with two others (or more) and see how "normal" you are and how "normal" your journey (mistakes, successes, realizations, etc) are. Sometimes we get blinded by our "issues" and feel we are on an island by ourselves. Friendships let us know that we are not alone. We have others to journey with.

But walking away from that conversation, my mind when to the stories we heard, as well as the ones Anne and I shared, and realized that many of them had to do with one thing: expectations. Because if expectations are not navigated through correctly, it can develop a massive amount of disappointment...especially early in marriage.

Have you ever been let down? You're probably picturing someone right now who has compromised your hope/expectations, and thus, giving you the feeling of disappointment. But understand: We've all been there. Anne and I visited "disappointment" often in our marriage, because, well, we've never been married before. Our expectations came from the only references we had: our family and upbringing. Some of you may have been married before and carry a whole other level of expectations that, you may not realize, have manipulated your thoughts and emotions. Regardless of where they come from, we need to work hard at attacking unrealistic expectations so that we can walk in marital health.

Steven Furtick once said, *"Frustration is born when our expectation doesn't match our experience."* It's a really great quote. I've adapted that into a teaching that I have shared (and drawn out) for so many couples to simply say:

Disappointment is the chasm between what we expected and what we experienced.

So many don't want to admit it, but marriage, by design, is supposed to have disappointments. Why? You are different in so many ways. From being different sexes to the social differences of your upbringing. Your differences will naturally produce some disappointments. My heart today is not to completely eliminate them. I don't think it's possible. But perhaps we can close the chasm between what you are expecting and experiencing and create a way to navigate through them in a healthy way.

1. **Be willing to lay your expectations down and, perhaps, admit they may not be realistic.** Humility produces a moldable marriage by showing that you don't have to have your way AND the fact that you don't have everything figured out. Proverbs 11:2 (NLT) says, "Pride leads to disgrace, but with humility comes wisdom." Humility to your heart likens to what farmers do to their fields in the spring; they churn the soil preparing it for seed, growth, and harvest.
2. **Set aside influences of discontent.** From media, to family, to friendships, what are the sources of discontent? What is influencing

your expectations that have you in a place unhappiness, envy, and displeasure? It's hard to feel full when you have outside sources trying to convince you that you are empty. Proverbs 13:25 (NLT), says "The godly eat to their hearts' content, but the belly of the wicked goes hungry." Why? Because their satisfaction isn't based upon what fulfills their lives but what satisfies a moment.

(NOTE: This is where Anne and I have discovered our fullness in Christ. Because if you do not find your fullness/contentment in Christ first, you will place expectations on your spouse, and others, they were never equipped to meet.)

Do you have outside influences of discontent? Keep them at arm's length and draw near to Christ. This leads to #3...

3. **Increasing your exposure edifying influences.** I'm not talking about chasing just what makes you "feel good." I'm talking about pursuing resources and people who can mentor you into healthier expectations that will fill you with hope. Think about the sun. The more exposure you get to it, the more of an effect it'll have on you (vitamin d, builds the immune system, can cure depression, etc.). Edifying influences that build you up will have the same effect.

4. **Get rid of the critical tongue.** The Gottman Institutes says criticism is "a wish disguised...a negative expression of real need." What needs to be done is to shut off the valve of criticism and to take responsibility for change. Instead of unloading all blame for unmet expectations, you begin to own it and help shoulder the responsibilities of developing a healthy expectation. Critical spirits fracture the oneness between you and your spouse. Introspective and humble hearts heal, fortify, and grow your marriage with realistic expectations.

5. **Form realistic goals together.** This can't be done by one or the other. By forming expectations that have been thought through AND prayed through by the BOTH of you, you will help set your marriage up for a journey of hope. Have periodic sit-downs

to not just cast vision for what to expect but also as a look back at how those expectations have been, or are being, met. Some great areas to look at and develop healthy expectations: Quality time together, home responsibilities, spiritual life, sexual relationship, money management, and parenting.

6. **Keep talking.** I believe couples face more disappointment than they need to experience because they have a "set it and forget it" with their expectations. Don't stop talking and shaping/adjusting what to expect. Communication is the oil of the engine of marriage. And the more you tend to what makes your marriage flow, the better you will traverse through issues of expectations and experiences and, thus, see less and less disappointment.

Today, start closing the chasm of disappointment by developing healthy expectations that will lead to healthy experiences. It begins by shaping your mind and communicating your heart. Don't lose hope. See your marriage through the eyes of God. Proverbs 23:18 (NLT) says, "There is surely a future hope for you, and your hope will not be cut off."

If you have Christ, you already have more than enough hope in Him. Embrace it. Walk in it.

- 27 -

One of the Few Things We Have in Common...and 5 Threats to Losing It

When thinking about our upcoming anniversary. I still don't understand what Anne saw (or sees) in me, but I'm very thankful she said "yes." Every year, marriage presents new challenges and every year I fall in a deeper love with her. There's no one else I would do life with.

Now that the sappiness is out of the way...

Looking at our overall relationship these past years, we have to admit how completely different we are. Someone just asked me about how compatible Anne and I are. I had to be honest...we don't have a ton of areas of "compatibility." I'm willing to bet that if we did the online dating 20 years ago, the online dating service would probably never match us up.

We have different interests
The interests we share, we do them differently (running, shows vs. movies, etc)
We grew up in completely different style homes.
We have different personality types.
We have completely different strengths.
We don't share the same love languages.
We don't grow spiritually the same way (the elements are similar but done differently).
We don't fully grasp what each other struggles with.

I have better taste in music than she does. (Really babe? Justin Bieber?)

So the question arises: Where are we alike (if at all)?

1. We both passionately love Jesus.
2. We both love to laugh.
3. We both have a strong resolve.

I like the word "resolve." You can call it "stubborn." You can use the word "determined." But whatever the synonym, Anne and I learned that having resolute mindset is a game-changer.

We refuse to paint an idealistic picture of a marriage without struggles (did you not read our list?). Like the seasons of a Michigan calendar year, good moments and challenging moments are what life brings you. It's the result of being a human that married a human. But it's the resolve that will push you through. It's your resolve that has made your mind up that regardless of what you face, you'll face it together and come out together on the other side.

But I promise (speaking from 18 years of experience) that there are things that want to weaken your resolve. Here are a few threats to look out for that want to weaken your resolve:

1. **Discouraging people.** I think of John 14 (NLT), when Jesus warns against having your resolve weakened by what you're facing rather than focusing upon Him. It happens to the best of us. And many times, it happens through people. I don't care if it's family, close friends, or your connections on social media, avoid people who will weaken your resolve to be a good spouse and/or see good in your spouse. Some people thrive on being critical without even desiring to be constructive. Find people who will encourage you. You need hope and not despair.

2. **Living on empty.** Anytime I've known people who have lost their resolve has been from a place of fatigue. Esau, in Genesis

25 (NLT), sells out the future of his family out of being tired and hungry. If you don't care for yourself spiritually, emotionally, and even physically, you are going to drain the strength of the resolve that helps you push through. Getting proper rest, spending quality time with the Lord, and living at a healthy pace will properly fuel the resolute mindset that helps a marriage push through.

3. **Neglecting the simple essentials.** Marriage isn't about "set it and forget it." It's a constant upkeep of what I consider the simple essentials. It's daily choices to build your resolve by facilitating:
   • Purposefully building healthy communication.
   • Serving your spouse's love language.
   • Constantly building your relationship with Christ
   • Engaging in a consistent sex life.
   • Learning how facilitate fun.

4. **Pornography.** The goal of pornography is to skew the authentic with fantasy. Whether it's visual porn (hyperbolized sexual imagery) or emotional porn (hyperbolized relational fantasy) the more open you are to it, the weaker your resolve will get as it will seed a false sense of dissatisfaction. Two of my biggest reasons is it causes an unhealthy view of the female body as well as unhealthy sexual expectations. Top it off with the addictive nature of porn devised to make you dependent upon it, you then have a monster that isn't worth the amount of space it will take up in your thoughts and the way it weakens your resolve.

5. **Toxic mindsets.** Hopelessness wants to break the back of your resolve. Like mixing too much sand into your concrete, it wants to make your resolute stance a bit more brittle than you expected. It's why scripture challenges us to stay clear of toxic mindsets like bitterness, rage, comparison, criticism, and unforgiveness. They say "you are what you eat." But a more biblical stance would be, "you are what you think." (Proverbs 23:7 NASV)

Your marriage doesn't need the compatibility that the world will say you need. But you do need to have a resolve.

I leave you with these final four challenges about your resolve:

1. Let your resolve will be driven from the heart of Jesus.
2. Let your resolve will be shown through the character of Jesus.
3. Resolve to seek AND be open to how the Holy Spirit wants to change you.
4. Resolve to not try to change your spouse but allow the Holy Spirit to change your spouse with the same amount of freedom you've given Him.

- 28 -

30-Something Lessons My Wife Taught Me: A Birthday Blog for Anne

To honor my wife, I thought I'd offer a quick lesson Anne has taught me for every year she's been alive:

1. It costs nothing to be kind.
2. The sun being out makes everything better.
3. Prayer isn't a moment; it's a lifestyle.
4. Swedish Fish and popcorn make TV shows better.
5. Don't mess with the "Monday Schedule."
6. There is never any reason for tickling. It should be a federal crime outlawed in all states.
7. Snacking is just like having a meal but is stretched out over the course of a few hours.
8. Listening is an art.
9. A home should be a safe-haven.
10. A smile can melt the hardest of hearts.
11. Encouragement can never be over-done.
12. There's always time for ice-cream.
13. Dating is never optional in marriage.
14. Weather is no excuse for not getting a run in.
15. The door, garage, and oven must be checked on before going to bed.
16. Pools > open bodies of water (because the fish will get you).

17. Quality running shoes leads to healthy running.
18. Accountability makes a world of difference.
19. Laughter is mandatory for a happy marriage.
20. A walk can calm the heart and clear the mind.
21. "Do you want a taco?" is a ridiculous question of epic proportion.
22. Football is only a game.
23. Only approved pictures get placed on social media.
24. Keep one ear bud out on a job so you can hear traffic when you are running.
25. The government/CIA/FBI is always watching. (#ParanoiaFrom TooManyTVShows)
26. There's no excuse...anyone can be generous.
27. Resilience is the key to perseverance.
28. A personal pain threshold is higher than you realize.
29. Your calling isn't my calling; my calling isn't yours.
30. Comparing yourself with others sucks the joy from your life.
30. something - Did I mention ice-cream...probably, but it bears repeating: There's always time for ice-cream.
30. something - Loving your children yet they drive you nuts is a constant tension.
30. something - It doesn't matter who got into bed first, Dave will always be the one to get up to turn off the light.
30. something - Sleeping-in is the best.
30. something - A quiet home is better than flowers.
30. something - Everyone should feel they are valued.
30. something - Everybody has time for someone.
30. something - A meaningful connection after a service can be just as impactful (if not more) as a Sunday sermon.

I love ya babe. I'm privileged to say that I've known more years of life with you than not. You're the best.

- 29 -

"Turn the Ship Around"
6 Small Actions to See Change
Happen in Your Marriage

I was watching a television show and they were discussing an oil tanker that had run aground. The narrative was building around a man named "Sam" that felt he could've done something about the issue long before the ship left the harbor. He is frustrated and calls First Lieutenant Emily Lowenbrau into his office to ask the question, "why couldn't they just stop and steer clear of the land?" Here's the dialogue (I promise there's a point to this):

Lt. Lowenbrau: "He dropped anchor."

Sam: "If he dropped anchor, why didn't he stop?"

Lt. Lowenbrau: "The anchor broke."

Sam: "Anchor's break?"

Lt. Lowenbrau: "I want you to guess something: a ship of this size and gross tonnage steaming at 18 knots, how long does it take to come to a complete stop the moment the bridge cuts the engines and throws the props into reverse?"

Sam: "I don't know...a couple football fields."

Lt. Lowenbrau: "Six miles. There's no anchor that stops that boat at 18 knots."

This has been a scene I have shared with quite a few couples over the past month. It's a simple illustration I use to show that, (1) marriages are not the easiest vessel to maneuver and (2) complete turnaround, often, does not happen immediately.

This is why so many couples call it quits. The issue that didn't develop overnight is expected to change overnight. You can't expect the issues that developed over years to go away overnight. Take purposeful and strategic steps forward. Remember: There are two broken individuals, with all of their habits and hurts, steaming ahead that need to see change in their own lives as well as their marriage.

Here's some simple actions to see turnaround:

1. **Show the same grace God has given you.** Every time I want to be bitter toward ANYONE (including my wife), this is the reminder I need. God's grace is not based upon how we see people deserving it. It's based upon the love of that Christ has for us. Ephesians 4:7 (ESV), says, "...grace was given to each one of us according to the measure of Christ's gift."

2. **Don't despise small beginnings.** I've seen so many spouses that have unrealistic expectations over the immediate progress of their spouse. Read Zechariah 4:10 (NLT). Don't look down on the small steps to turnaround. Is your spouse "there" yet? Nope. But neither are you.

3. **Stop comparing.** So many journeys are screwed up by looking at the wrong route. Hebrews 12 (ESV) says, "fix your eyes on Jesus" not "fix your eyes on your best friend's marriage." I look to others to encourage me. I lean on mentors to challenge me. But the direction or health of my marriage doesn't come from fixating on someone else's journey. It comes from fixing my eyes on Jesus and following His lead.

4. Don't stop fostering hope. How do you do that? Find ways to encourage your spouse. Find people who are encouraging to be around. Shut out the negative voices. The same God that saw a hope for a broken nation (Jeremiah 29:11 ESV) sees hope for your future. But you need to take the necessary steps to foster it.

5. **Celebrate often.** Weight watchers taught me something that I have never forgotten: celebrate every success. That meant it didn't matter if I lost 1 pound or 1 ounce. It was all cause for celebration. Philippians 4:4 (ESV) challenges us to "rejoice always" which indicates that it's not based upon our circumstances. It's a direction you place your mind. Celebrate every step, great or small, and learn to infuse your marriage with joy.

6. **Do what you used to do.** In the book of Revelation, Jesus dealt with a church that was going through the motions but didn't have the love they needed. The simple instructions were to "repent" (turn away from what they were doing) and "do the things you did at first." Think about the things you did when you first fell in love...THEN DO THEM!!! It's sounds a bit too simple but it's an amazing way to see "turnaround" develop as well as passion grow in your marriage.

The old cliché says, "The titanic doesn't turn on a dime." Marriage is no different. The healthiest marriages I know have not only faced storms but take careful, strategic steps forward.

...And most of those steps are simpler than you realize. Keep fighting for your marriage. Keep fostering hope.

- 30 -

"I wish you were more like..."...and 6 other lines we shouldn't say in marriage

---

"Death and life are in the power of the tongue, and those who love it will eat its fruits." Proverbs 18:21 (ESV)

I always, say, "Communication is the oil of the engine of marriage." And just like the car you drive, you cannot afford to use the same oil for great lengths of time. Oil must be changed every 3000 or so miles to keep the engine running at peak performance. Thus, as we move forward in our marriage, we should always keep an eye on our communication to see if our communication needs to be refreshed. Why? Through the seasons of life, you change. Shocking enough, so will your spouse. The ways you address and respond to each other should always be on our radar as marriage becomes the place to endlessly learn to communicate.

I know marriage is much more than communication, but how many marital issues would be erased or solved if we just learned to communicate in a more healthy manner? Our almost 18 years have taught us that it's not a matter of if we disagree, but when we do, how will we handle it? Here's a simple rule: We should never quit and always communicate until you reach the other side. This, of course, takes hard work and dedication... and a few bits of sound wisdom on how to resolve things more healthily wouldn't hurt either. Thus, this blog.

It's impossible to define everything everyone should or shouldn't say in every situation.

However, there are a couple of phrases/words that we've discovered are usually unhelpful for marriage:

"You always/never..." Absolute statements like "you always..." or "you never..." are something Anne and I continue to try to remove from our marriage. I think we've done well. In fact, when we are joking with each other, we'll usually use this phrase as if to tell the other person, "when you hear this, it's never about anything of actual consequence."

The problem with absolute statements is that, first, they're rarely true when speaking of behavior, and, second they are usually hurtful. The only thing we accomplish by using this kind of talk is sowing seeds of repeated failure. It kills any positive momentum, and it's a reminder of past failures. Absolute statements say more about who's saying them then they do about whom they're directed at. To shoot straight with you, absolute statements are just plain lazy. This is an easy one to resort to in an argument. It cuts quick and deep, it's a low blow, and they're a poor way to verbalize the real issues at hand.

By being specific and purposeful with your language, you can actually move forward together instead of accusing one another. Removing absolute statements from your marriage diction will do wonders.

"I wish you were more like..." Comparison isn't a marriage builder; it's a marriage killer. It is disrespectful and damaging. Any time you find yourself comparing your spouse to another husband or wife, you are comparing their highlight reel to your behind-the-scenes. It is always based on the partial truth of somebody else's reality Comparison creates an unfair and unrealistic standard to live up to.

Nobody likes being compared to someone else. Whether it's a friend, a stranger, or a family member, comparison will break hearts and kill

MOSAIC MARRIAGE | 121

marriage momentum. Nothing makes me feel smaller than when I'm unscrupulously compared to someone "greater than" me. Feeling that kind of small is ok, I guess, but only if it's relation to Jesus. May Jesus be the only person we compare with and let the be with ourselves as we ask him to increase and us decrease.

"I'm sorry, but…" I understand can be hard to apologize. But using the word "but" on the end of an apology is giving yourself permission to do something you probably shouldn't be doing in the first place. Some people are more stubborn than others (like me). But when you do apologize, leave it at "I'm sorry." If you add the word "but" with any explanation, valid or not, it negates any form of apology that preceded it. Apologies should be sincere and should bring finality to the conversation. If you're not done sharing your feelings, then don't apologize!

"Whatever!" The ultimate shutdown response when you've run out of words. But even more than that, it becomes an easy immature go-to. What this says is, "I don't really want to deal with the situation" and/ or "I refuse to talk about this."

The word "Whatever" is the arch-enemy of biblical reconciliation. By dismissing disagreements with "whatever", you're essentially stating that you don't care enough about the person or disagreement to discuss further. Remember, "Love never quits. Love is patient, kind, not easily angered, and always perseveres" (1 Corinthians 13). Please understand, it's not that "whatever" is a bad word, it's just usually used in moments when love isn't at its best. Ditching "whatever" from your marriage vocabulary will force to either, first, explain why you're OK with dismissing the conversation, or, second, explain why you're truly ok with whatever.

"I'm fine." (Here's a personal favorite.) Now this one is tricky. Whoever is the more emotional member (not necessarily the female) will use this as a hint of deeper things going on. What is troublesome about

"fine" is it's usually a passive aggressive approach to announcing that "everything isn't fine and you need to pick up on the signal."

Seeing that your spouse isn't a mind-reader, I challenge you to remove "fine" from your vocabulary and look for more constructive opportunities mixed with clear open dialogue to convey what the issues at hand is.

"...just sayin'..." This is the arrogant jab at the end of a statement as if you want to flaunt your right to say what you want. But note: Just because you have a right doesn't make it right. Just as much as pride will destroy the work of Christ in your life, pride will destroy what Christ desires to do in your marriage. The desire to tack this onto your statement should be the red flag that what will proceed "just sayin'" may not set your conversation up for a healthy and constructive interaction.

"Divorce..." Whether is joking or serious, I think it's dangerous for couples use the word "divorce" in reference to their marriage. I believe marriage only works if divorce is not an option. It's looking at your life together as if there's no back door. That way you'll both be committed to working through anything.

The greatest enemy we've seen at play in marriage is simply giving up by mentally, emotionally, physically, and spiritually check-out of the marriage. How can you work something out if one person leaves or refuses to engage? Divorce is just that: giving up on the marriage.

Using the word "divorce" potentially introduces the idea of a terrible possibility into your marriage. No matter how you slice it, divorce is marital death...and a painful one at that. I implore you, remove "divorce" from your vocabulary. Don't use it as a threat, comedic relief, or otherwise. Perhaps you should divorce yourself from using "divorce."

Words are essential to healthy communication. And I hope I've made a compelling case for why you should remove some phrases and words from your marriage.

Proverbs 18:21 (ESV) "Death and life are in the power of the tongue, and those who love it will eat its fruits." Be selective with your words. There are two things in this life you can never get back once used, words and time.

Use your words to give life. And your marriage will feast on the fruits of them (words).

- 31 -

"The 15-Minute Marriage"
Marriage Transformation
One Minute at a Time

I'm a sucker for infomercials. They can memorize me by their loud hosts with their crazy contraptions. And if the host has an English accent, they can practically sell me anything (I have issues).

Most of these advertisements have a certain amount of easy actions to take.

- 3 seconds to a fruit smoothie
- 4 steps to set it and forget it
- 5 decisions to feel better about yourself
- 2 steps to hang...whatever it is you want to hang

What I don't want you to think is that I'm giving you a "formula." What today's marriage blog is about is simple actions to produce healthy habits in a Christ-centered marriage. And my thought today:

If I can help someone consistently (every day) dedicate 15 purposeful minutes of their entire day to their marriage, I believe they're marriage will be completely transformed.

Take a look...I've given you 15 items that take 60 seconds or less to accomplish. But these minute-long action steps are laced with deep seeded health.

1. **Take a minute to thank God for your spouse.** Gratitude fosters humility. Thank God for your spouse's salvation (or for providing a salvation for you to deliver to him/her). Then start listing things that you are thankful to God for in them.
   o Here's some ideas: his/her kindness, generosity, parenting, leadership, work ethic, great sex (yes, it's okay to thank God for sex), ministry, tidiness, resolve, and patience.

2. **Take a minute to send random texts during the day to connect or give a simple "I love you."** A text takes a matter of 5-10 seconds-ish so this pans out anywhere from 4 (for slower texters) to 10 (faster texters).

3. **Take a minute to think of a way to serve your spouse and put it onto your calendar so you don't forget.** It could be as simple as "load the dishwasher before she asks." Remember: the little things matter.

4. **Take a minute to connect to your spouse with something that will make him/her smile.** Doesn't matter if it's a meme you found on social media. Maybe it's a video clip. Get your spouse smiling.

5. **Take a minute to speak hope over your marriage.** Read a scripture over your spouse and pray it over him/her.
   o Get a bible app. Usually it has a feature called "verse of the day." Biblegateway.com has verse of the day too.

6. **Take a minute to encourage your spouse.** One moment up building up your spouse can make a world of difference.

7. **Take a minute to think of and initiate some quality time the two of you can do together.**

8. **Take a minute to pray over something important to your spouse.** How do you know what is on your spouse's heart? Ask him/her. Think of what they're gonna think when he/she discovers that he/she is in your daily prayer.

9. **Take a minute to physically embrace your spouse (especially if you're not a physical touch person...it'll shock him/her).** Show PDA towards your spouse: holding hands, a touch on the shoulder, a kiss on the cheek, or pat on the bottom.

10. **Take a minute to think of a conversation you SHOULD have.** A ten-minute conversation can head off a ten-hour conflict

11. **Take a minute to ask God to reveal how you can be a better spouse.** Let the Holy Spirit show you some areas of growth. When He does, walk in obedience.

12. **Take a minute to ask God to fill your heart with His desires for your marriage.**

13. **Take a minute to appreciate your spouse.** Look at the world through his/her eyes and understand what they're dealing with and going through. It'll help you connect and come along side of him/her.

14. **Take a minute to say "goodbye" the right way.** When departing from your spouse, refuse to leave unless there has been an expression of love.

    o   Our habit, no matter our mood, we kiss and say "I love you." When that doesn't happen, we know something is up and needs to be dealt with. Usually it's my crappy attitude.

15. **Take a minute to address a need or situation at hand.** Need forgiveness...ask. Need to grant forgiveness...give. Need humility...walk in it. Need to be listen...shut up. Need to be heard...speak up (in appropriate tones).

That's it. 15 minutes, that don't have to be done all at once, will transform you and, thus transform your spouse. Look at that list and you'll see:

1. Out of those 15, five of them center around praying for your spouse.

2. None of them put you in a place of superiority over your spouse but pure humility.

3. Five of them initiate necessary conversation points that can dismantle assumption, confusion, and disagreements.
4. Four of them put you in a place to think like and for your spouse. That gets us to get out of our selfish mindsets.
5. Lastly, none of them are dependent upon your spouse doing anything. Let it begin with you regardless of whether he/she reciprocates them.

I challenge you to step up and add 15 minutes of your day to your marriage. I promise: try it for 30 days and if you don't see change in you, your spouse, and/or the both of you, I'll give your money back and pay for the shipping (sad reconnection to my previous illustration).

Health is simple, not easy, simple. It's just takes one intentional at a time. Ask the Lord for patience. Receive his strength. Follow through His leading with obedience.

- 32 -

"Complement-less Marriages" 6 Simple Ways to Complement Your Spouse

---

"The one who blesses others is abundantly blessed; those who help others are helped." Proverbs 11:25 (MSG)

Who doesn't like a complement? It's very rare (and I mean rare) where you legitimately find someone who doesn't enjoy (not necessarily seeking after) a genuine complement.

I'm not talking about flattering someone. The purpose of flattery is to get a reaction or a response that will directly benefit the person giving the so-called "complement." A true complement is selflessly giving for the purpose of affirming and encouraging someone with zero manipulation. Edification should be the only motivation behind complements.

When it comes to marriage, it seems that the longer people are together, the more apt they are to take complements for granted. They seem so small, and to some so insignificant, but they're a huge need in your relationship. One of my favorite books to use in premarital counseling is Gary and Barbara Rosberg's, "The 5 Sex Needs of Men & Women." In it both him and his wife discuss the top 5 needs of both genders. Of the five, two needs are shared amongst both sexes: Connection (purposefully linking into your spouse's world) and Affirmation (offering emotional support or encouragement).

Think about it, genuine and meaningful compliments touch at least two of the most intimate needs us as human beings have. That's the power of a complements. The key to this, and it may seem difficult, is the mentality behind it. Yes I want you both to go after this. But I want our mindset to be very personal. Let it start with you. If you go into this complementing thing waiting for him/her to start it and/or reciprocating it, you're more about flattery than the true complement. Make this both a personal strategy as well as a couple's strategy.

Marriage issues are never a quick fix. But sometimes it's the small changes that help turn the Titanic around.

Here's you go...6 easy ways to compliment your spouse:

1. **Go After the Effort.** Guys, she may not care about your vehicle, hobby, or sporting interest, but if she asks, it means she's trying to connect with you. Ladies, don't think to yourself, "he doesn't really care." He does and he's trying. It may not look or sound the way you want but he's attempting to connect with you.

The quickest way to shut down any progress in a marriage is to look pessimistically at attempts to step forward. I've always counseled parents to praise the efforts of their kids and not necessarily just the accomplishment. Why don't we do that with our spouse? Why do so many of us jump at the criticism before gratitude and encouragement?

2. **Look for the obvious.** Don't be the person that says, "he/she already knows how I feel." From his/her role in the family to how he/she loves Jesus, bring out the obvious things.

Both men and women deal with the lure of constant comparison with the people in their lives. We are faced with constant changes physically, emotionally, and mentally. Don't take ANY obvious complement for granted.

3. **Go after the not-so-obvious.** Guys, your wife loves details. Saying "you look nice" doesn't cut it. Look beyond the surface words and specifically point things out. She works hard on details. You should work hard on noticing them. Ladies, get after what he is into. You may not care specifically about it, but you care about him. Asking and encouraging will bring you into his world. When you two get past the surface, it speaks value to your spouse. Ask yourself, "what does he/she think I don't notice." Go after that.

4. **Get spiritual.** When was the last time you complimented his/her desire for a deeper relationship with God? I've met too many spouses that have an intimidation of their partner's spirituality. Get over that and encourage their walk with Christ. Feed your spouse's every spiritual step toward Jesus with high levels of encouragement. That doesn't mean that you are doing the same bible studies and having 3-hour prayer services together before you go to bed. Celebrate what Jesus is doing in your marriage and each other's lives.

5. **Be frequent.** Please don't use the words, "I've already said that." I'm not sure that I've ever met a couple who complement/encourage too much. Making a habit of affirming your spouse keeps, what Gary Chapman would say, your husband's/wife's "love tank" filled. Far too many affairs have happened because someone stepped into a void left by an unmet need. Leave no place for anyone to out-complement you when it comes to your spouse. Do it often and do it well.

6. **Leave no strings attached.** Ever met that person that gave you a compliment with the expectation you were going to give one back. It's self-serving and manipulative. Pour encouragement into your spouse with zero expectations back. Why? It fosters humility. It removes pride. The right motives are developed and lived.

Do you want it reciprocated back? Sure you do. But edification without strings sets down "self" in order to place your spouse's needs first. Imagine if you had two individuals doing this at the same time in their marriage. That'd be the craziest display of marital health you've ever seen.

Proverbs 11:25 (MSG) The one who blesses others is abundantly blessed; those who help others are helped.

Have any one of us "arrived." Not at all. Whenever I feel like I'm good at it, either I take it for granted or, out of my humanity, I begin to attach strings. You're human which means your broken. But don't let that be your excuse not to take intentional, self-initiated steps toward building up your spouse. When you step forward to bless your spouse, the natural outcome is you and your marriage get blessed (Proverbs 11:25 MSG). Don't be stingy. Don't neglect it. Speak out and build up your spouse.

Again, don't expect everything to change overnight or assume marriage issues are a quick fix. Take it a moment at a time. Take it one word of edification at a time. And watch your humility and encouragement change the atmosphere of your marriage.

- 33 -

"Warning Shots"
10 subtle actions your marriage
needs to pay attention to

You've opened my ears so I can listen. Psalm 40:6 (MSG)

I'm an aficionado of military movies. And there's certain lines and terms that you can count on hearing frequently. For some reason, especially in movies involving ships, you'll hear the term: warning shot.

A warning shot is a military and/or police term describing an intentionally harmless shot toward the opposition. The intention of the shot is to get the attention of the party at hand letting them know you mean business. The warning shot doesn't harm or hurt anyone. It's what I call the "attention grabber." It tells the opposing person that if you do not heed the "warning shot", consequences will follow.

I'm not being a proponent of firing a shot, both literal and physical, at/toward your spouse. But there are subtle things that happen in a marriage that are the "attention grabbers" of your relationship. Many times, these are not intentionally done by a spouse. They're the subtle responses to situations that are not completely healthy. But to ignore these "warning shots" is to inviting the issuing circumstances.

10 warning shots to take notice of:

1. **Taking for granted "The Big 5."** They consist of:
   - "I love you."
   - "Will you forgive me?"
   - "I forgive you."
   - "Thank you."
   - "You're welcome."

2. **Love languages are becoming a side issue.** I think couples should monitor the changes in their love languages as they get older. The seasons of life change you. What used to speak to your spouse may not speak to them now. Take time to read, talk, pray, and discover each other all over again. The pursuit will feed the passion.

3. **The schedule doesn't allow you to worship and prayer together.** We are more than physical beings. We are spiritual as well. When the two became one, the two were meant to experience everything together...including worship. If the schedule is preventing time of spiritual refreshing, something needs to change. When you can't remember the last time you haven't prayed together, served together, or worshiped together, they're subtle hints that spiritual intimacy needs to be a priority.

4. **The decisions you used to make together are now being decided without the other.** This is a sign that communication and unified decision-making are beginning to break down. It always starts off with the little things.

5. **Sex isn't happening.** My love language is "Physical Touch" so this isn't a subtle hint. But for those of you who are not driven physically, if sex isn't happening in a healthy frequency (no magic number for that), it's a definite sign that something needs to change. The heart should drive the mood. Both spouses should possess the heart of a servant to make sure that the most intimate needs of their spouse is being served. As I've always said, "you are the only one that can meet that need in your spouse."

6. **There's much more tolerance for what you never tolerated before.** There's freedom in Christ and there's just cashing in on Godly standards. Your entertainment, conversations, thought-life, and private time should have healthy Godly boundaries. If they're not attended to, it amazing me what gets past them and desires to take root in our lives.

7. **"This is your problem not mine." becomes a common line.** This is one of many quotes that shows the breakdown of oneness in a marriage. "Mine" and "yours" are natural words used by couples whose unity is beginning to erode away. Take notice on how much they're being used and in the context they're being used. Take a step back and realize: you are in this together. Make sure your words follow suit.

8. **Date night?** I hear couples joke "Does that happen anymore?" and it makes me cringe every time. When you can't remember when it's happened last, it's a sure sign that you desperately need time alone. It doesn't have to cost much if anything at all. Take a walk. Go on a drive. Do something together.

9. **Kids are higher priority than the marriage.** Your children are a temporary assignment; marriage is not. I know you have such a short window of time to raise your children. I'm a firm believer that kids are a high priority...just behind my spouse. I don't neglect or ignore my kids. BUT...my wife is a higher priority. She needs to know that. My kids need to see that. This is why so many people get divorced after 20-25 years of marriage. Everything was poured into the kids and nothing into the marriage.

10. **There's more talk about what you DON'T have than what you DO have.** Envy is a killer of joy in your marriage. It wants to guide your eyes and heart to what others have and what you lack. You end up forgetting the blessings of God because you can't see them past all of the "stuff" that should be yours. "If only I/we had it." is a lie. Why? Because when you do get "it", you'll still continue to say that line.

My prayer for you is that of Psalms 40:6 (MSG), that you would be able to say, God "opened my ears so I can listen." Ask the Lord to open up your 5 senses to hear the subtle things that you haven't noticed before. If you see these things, they are the attention grabbers that are screaming at you saying, "it's time to attend to your marriage."

Don't grow deaf to the "warning shots." Open up your senses and listen.

- 34 -

"Razor Sharp"
6 Ways to keep your marriage sharp

From the beginning of this, please note something: Marriage is hard work. In saying that, I want to pose a question:

Are we working too hard on our marriage?

Before you fire off emails, posts, rebuttals, etc at me, I want to work out a thought that came out the other day. It stemmed from a simple saying:

Work smarter; not harder.

When my son turned 10, he got his first pocket knife. He's seen me whittle before (I'm not very good) and he's been wanting to do it too. I wanted to make sure it was sharp and it stayed sharp. Anne was concerned he was going to lose an appendage keeping it sharp. But I explained something key: The sharper you keep your knife, the easier it is to work on the project and, thus, less likely to get hurt. So, often I'd have Ethan bring me his knife and we'd take a few moments to sharpen his blade. I know it frustrated him to stop his project for something that seemed so small, but little corrections to the blade made all of the difference. Struggling with a dull knife invites motions and angles that can lead to injuries.

Marriage is no different. Some of you are working hard on some areas with "dull blades." You find yourself getting hurt in conversations and conflicts. You leave moments together with "nicks" on your heart. I want to help you work smarter. It doesn't remove the hard work, but why make hard work harder? It's time to regain your "edge." It's time to step back and make some small, intentional moves that can keep your marriage sharp.

1. **Monitor the Love Languages.** The longer we're together, the more apt we take communication for granted. We assume our spouse should just "know" what's going on and/or what we are thinking. So we go on "business as usual" not realizing the sharpness of our talking has been dulled because we either stopped speaking appropriately to our spouse or didn't realize that the season of life has changed our spouse's love language. Some of you are working incredibly hard communicating to your spouse and it's not working. Could it be that your speaking the wrong language? Could it be that tones and mannerisms are dulling the blade of your communication?

Sharpening Tips: Read "5 Love Languages" together. Be a student of how your spouse and how he/she communicates. Find opportunities to pour into what speaks to them and not you.

2. **Keep in touch with each other.** There's no excuse in today's age of tech to not have steady communication. From a regular time to go over the upcoming week to having daily time to talk about the simple things of the day. These are quality moments that keep couples sharp and prepared. It's amazing how a 15-minute talk can keep a razor's edge to your marriage and prevent unnecessary conflict. It'll astound you how a few texts during the day can prepare hearts for intimacy. Keeping in touch doesn't take much but it is "jaw-dropping" how much benefit it brings for such simplistic actions. Remember, quantity doesn't equate to quality. A hand-full of quality daily moments can make you sharper than once-in-a-while quantity connection.

Sharpening Tips: Get a google calendar to share so that appointments/schedules are understood. Text to connect not to keep track. Randomly direct message, Facebook message, etc. your spouse about your day. Random "I love you" messages will do more than you realize.

3. **Have Fun.** I seriously can't write about this enough. It's, quite possibly, the area of marriage both husband and wife take for granted the most. It doesn't seem necessary for some. It seems to be the first thing to be sacrificed. Yet it might be one of the most spiritual acts you do together. Fun doesn't have to cost anything!!! It can be so simple AND cheap. When you have fun...

- passionate feelings are rekindled
- defenses are lowered and the real you comes out
- intimacy is stoked
- you remember why you got married

Couples that don't consistently have fun are working with a dulled-bland and have to work harder AND rarely get the results of couples who consistently feed their marriage fun.

Sharpening Tips: Schedule, as best as you can, a regular "date" time for you two. Look for random moments during mundane weeks to break away for a quick date (Anne and I do froyo). Take turns on who plans the dates.

4. **Show appreciation.** There's not a person existing that doesn't like to feel appreciated. From gratitude to complements, don't assume your spouse knows that you appreciate them. Kind words and encouragement will build the infrastructure of servanthood in your marriage. Appreciation sharpens the heart of humility. It creates in atmosphere where spouses look for ways to meet the needs of their partner. Refusal to show appreciation dulls the joy in serving. That which was once a labor of love is now a job of obligation.

Sharpening Tips: Show gratitude for the not-so-obvious/normal things in life (doing well at their job, how well they're doing as a parent, etc). Using your spouse's love language, express random appreciation that will benefit him/her more than you. Drop a note. Make a favorite meal.

5. **Have a consistent love life.** PLEASE DON'T SKIP over this if you have a lower sex-drive than your spouse. Please don't diminish this because it's not a big deal for you. Regular (defined by the two of you) sexual connection creates health on every level (physical, emotional, mental, spiritual). Like working with a dulled blade, frustration, confusion, and hurt are easy byproducts of an inconsistent love life. Sexual needs are the only needs that NO ONE ELSE can supply in your spouse but you.

Sharpening Tips: Talk frustrations through regardless of how previous talks went. See intimacy beyond sex by fostering healthy touches and communication that are not laced with sexual expectations. Plan out nights for intimacy and keep it consistent (that might sound unromantic, but for those who struggle with their libido, it actually helps them be ready on every level).

6. **Don't tolerate bitterness.** Call it bitterness. Call it unforgiveness. Call it a grudge. It really doesn't matter what name it goes by, it's poison. It will be cancerous to your marriage. Bitterness will do more than dull blade of your marriage, it'll rust it though. It's designed to destroy you both. Sharp couples know that bitterness is never worth it and work to keep their blade free of it. Razor sharp couples make sure that forgiveness is asked for and granted. These type of marriage live life free of the bondage that bitterness wants to lead to. Are you keeping score on each other's faults? Are you trying to repay someone for their mistakes? You're not just hurting them...you're hurting you and the marriage. Do not put up with unforgiveness. Release it to the Lord and leave it with him.

Sharpening Tips: Forgive in proportion to how God has forgiven you. Get counsel on deep-seeded hurts. Communicate your act of forgiveness to your spouse. If you're the one who messed up, ask for forgiveness AND forgive yourself.

I know I could add more, but these are the few that have been weighing on my heart. With your marriage, keep it sharp. You will find yourself working smarter than working harder. And by doing that, you'll see yourself "whittling/sculpting" a marriage that reflects an image of God to be a testimony to the world around you.

- 35 -

Marital Catchphrases – Part 1
"Yes Dear!"

"Careful words make for a careful life; careless talk may ruin everything." Proverbs 13:3 (MSG)

I'll share with you a secret about my marriage. Anne and I talk in "catchphrases" from TV show and movies. I don't know when it began, but somewhere early in our 15 years of marriage, phrases from favorite shows and actors started coming through our mouths sparking the connection and laughter we feel is necessary to keep our marriage healthy. Why? First, we take the scripture at face value when we are told that laughter is a medicine (Proverbs 17:22 NTL). Secondly, it's been proven that people who laugh are healthier (Wish I could find that article right now but you'll have to take my word it).

Last September, I had come across an article about the Top 60 Catchphrases from TV. What these simple one-liners are, are quotes that you not only hear consistently from the characters, but the "phrases" are associated with the character's development in the show. Some of them are funny the first 50 times. The problem, if you watch a show over and over, the "catchphrase" becomes white noise. It kinda loses something because it is so predictable. After reading through, a marriage blog series began to form. I asked myself the question:

Do I have marriage "catchphrases" that I use?

Over the years, there are things that I say that I've been stating so often that it's become white noise. In other words, these statements don't carry the punch or effect it used to have. What ends up happening is my actions (or lack thereof) negate the effectiveness of the phrases I use with my wife. Something needs to change.

I asked Anne which catchphrase to start with. She hit a homerun with the answer:
"Yes Dear"
"Can you take out the garbage?" "Yes Dear."
"Can you bring me _____?" "Yes Dear."
"The kids are screaming at each other. Do something about it!" "Yes Dear."

What is communicated by that two-word phrase? If you're in the "Honeymoon Phase" of marriage, "Yes Dear" means "I'm thrilled to do this for you...by the way, we're going to have sex later." A few years after that, the meaning usually changes to "I'm saying these two words to pacify you till you either forget you asked me for something or you go and do it yourself."

Yes, Dear.

We throw it out so casually. It, if we're not careful, can become a cop-out to actual conversation. Anne made a great point this morning. "Yes, Dear" is almost a mockery of your spouse. It an easy out for actually taking the time to give open and honest communication to your spouse. For example:
"Can you take care of something for me?"
"Yes, Dear."

(Either one spouse is disgruntled because their spouse didn't get the task done in the time expected or the other spouse is frustrated that he/she had to stop what they were doing to get the tack accomplished.)

Perhaps the new response should turn into:
"Can you take care of something for me?"
"That shouldn't be a problem. I'm in the middle of something now. Can I take care of it a bit later?"

BOTH parties need to step back out of their agenda and have respect enough to stand back and think before engaging.

If you don't want a "Yes, Dear" reply:

1. **Timing is everything.** Make sure you have your spouse's' complete attention. If you don't think you have it, simply ask.
2. **Clearly define what is being asked.** Make sure your spouse knows what you require as well as timing. You cannot blame your spouse if you haven't communicated clearly.
3. **Be polite.** The longer we are married the more we take each other for granted. Don't stop saying "please" and "thank you."
4. **If you get "yes dear", ask your spouse what the "yes dear" means.** What you should hear back is "I heard that you need _____ done by (certain time) today." Don't let the catchphrase pacify you. Make sure you know that you've been heard.

For you "Yes Dear" people (like myself):

1. **What is my spouse actually asking for?** Look past the surface. Your spouse may be wanting attention, affection, time, or simply want to be heard more than actually getting a task done.
2. **What is the emotion driving it?** Is he/she frustrated? Is there a sense of urgency? If you spouse is urgent about something but you refuse to sense that urgency, you're telling your spouse that you don't have the time to validate their feelings and you are asking for the same treatment. Don't just hear the request, listen to the feeling behind the request.
3. **How important is this to my spouse?** We always want what's important to us to be important to our spouse. It's a wonderful

fairy-tale scenario. But reality is: so many couples struggle because their only urgency rests in what they selfishly feel is urgent. I will get into a zone watching a football game. Anne will get into a zone when she is organizing. It may be a silly illustration, but we have both been frustrated with the other because we were bothered at inconvenient moments. In our "zones", we refuse to listen to the importance of what our spouse is saying.

Back to the scripture we started this whole blog with. Proverbs 13:3 (MSG) says "Careful words make for a careful life; careless talk may ruin everything." A careless approach to marital longevity involves the use of over-used catchphrases that can be detrimental to a healthy life with our spouse. Take a step back. Examine your words. Ask for forgiveness. Communicate effectively.

- 36 -

Marital Catchphrases – Part 2
"I'm Sorry."

"Careful words make for a careful life; careless talk may ruin everything." Proverbs 13:3 (MSG)

My sole goal today is simple: I want you to stop saying *"I'm sorry."*

Relax...get ya some tea (Moroccan is my fav)...and I'll explain.

"Did you break this?" "I'm sorry."
"You bought what?!?" "I'm sorry."
"I can't believe you said that to the kids?" "I'm sorry."
"You invited your mother?" "I'm sorry."

This simple phrase that our parents taught us so well has been so over-used and abused. I think of when my parents were trying to teach my sister to say those words. I remember it well. Rachael hit me. My parents saw her and sternly told her, "Don't you ever hit your brother. If it happens, you need to say *'I'm sorry.'*" What my parents said and what Rachael heard were two different things. My parents were trying to teach her remorse and manners. Rachael heard something else. She began to hit me while quickly following up the punch with a quick *"I'm sorry."* It got so bad she was actually saying *"I'm sorry"* while her fist was flying through the air. To her very young mind, it was the escape from all consequence and responsibilities that were connected with her actions.

We adults are not all that different.

The more I counsel, the more I hear the same very disturbing words: "*When my spouse says they're sorry, it doesn't mean anything to me anymore.*"

How do you get to that point? It's elementary my dear Watson (sorry...I've been watching Sherlock). It's the same mentality that my preschool sister used that we still try to enforce today. If I say "*I'm sorry*," then things will go back to normal and I don't have to face any consequences and take greater responsibility over my life. We use these simple words as band aids for wounds that need serious treatment. The words "*I'm sorry*" have been used over and over and over and over...

...till the hold vertically no meaning.

It becomes a worse situation when that spouse really does have remorse over their actions and their spouse cannot take their word for it. It didn't have any meaning before. It doesn't have any meaning to them now.

Psalm 34:13 (NASV) says, "Keep your tongue from evil and your lips from speaking deceit." If you and I are professing remorse with our lips but do not possess it in our hearts and our actions, we are not apologizing. We are simply speaking deceit. Something needs to change. Something must be transformed.

Here's some help: **First**, confront the issue. James 5:16 (ESV) tells us that confession leads to healing. Talk to your spouse about the revelation you've come to. Confess your deceit and bring it into the light. Quit hiding it and letting the darkness grow something that doesn't belong in your life.

Secondly, Apologize correctly. Get rid of the words "I'm sorry." Somebody taught us something a long time ago about apologies. Take out the words "*I'm sorry*" and replace them with "*Will you forgive me?*"

There is an amazing difference. There's something about the words *"Will you forgive me?"* that demands a **two-fold action**:

1. **For the person apologizing, there's an action of humility and recognition that what you've done was wrong and hurtful.** You are humbling yourself by removing excuse and positioning yourself and your spouse for healing.
2. **For the spouse receiving the apology, there is a reciprocated action demanded.** There is only TWO responses to the words "Will you forgive me?" You will either hear "no" or "yes I forgive you." There's no other option. If you say, "yes I forgive you," then you are position yourself in a place of acting and living in forgiveness.

I remember quite a few years ago, Anne had done something wrong. What I remember about the situation wasn't what she had done to me. It was the end of the skirmish that sticks in my mind. We were driving and she looked over at me and said, *"Honey, will you forgive me?"*

My reply, *"Yes."*

After about a 3 second pause, she said again, *"Honey, do you forgive me?"* I knew what she was asking. We had agreed some time before that we would always apologize to each other in that manner. We felt it positioned our marriage to walk in forgiveness. To express the words *"I forgive you"* would put the onus on the other to let go of anger and bitterness and ACTUALLY forgive. I remember not wanted to say it. I wanted to linger in my anger...

...but that's just it isn't it? We need to let go. We need to forgive without stipulation the way Christ forgives us.

One more time, *"Will you forgive me?" "Yes babe...I forgive you."*
This stuff may not be a big deal to you. But the more "catchphrases" we can eliminate, the more we can position our marriages to walk in the heath that the Lord has designed for us to live in.

- 37 -

Marital Catchphrases – Part 3
"Don't Worry About It."

"Careful words make for a careful life; careless talk may ruin everything."
Proverbs 13:39 (MSG)

"How much did you spend at the store?" "Don't worry about it!"
"What are you looking at on your computer?" "Don't worry about it!"
"What did you say to your mother?" "Don't worry about it!"
"When are you going to be home?" "Don't worry about it!"

(I can almost hear the temperature of tempers rising...you've heard this "catchphrase" before haven't you?)

It was about 9 or so years ago and we were on vacation in Florida with my entire family. My parents had rented a hug home for the entire family to stay in. On our first night there, Anne had woken up to find me missing from the bed. She walked out to the living room area to find me sitting in the dark on my computer intently staring at the screen. All I heard was *"What in the world are you doing at 4am?"* My reply? *"Don't worry about it. Go back to bed."*

With all the volume she could muster without waking up my parents and my sister's family, I heard these words, *"DON'T YOU DARE TELL ME THAT!!! I'M YOUR ACCOUNTABILITY AND YOU ARE GOING TO TELL ME RIGHT NOW WHAT YOU ARE LOOKING AT!"*

I hung my head in shame. I looked up at her and showed her my screen. *"Babe, Marty and I are against each other in our Fantasy Baseball Championship and I had to wake up and get my players before he gets up...I gotta beat him!"*

The only reply she gave was, *"This is stupid...I'm going back to bed."*

When you hear those words *"Don't worry about it"*, what do you hear? (I'm not talking about the casual response to a silly situation: *"I ordered you a Coke instead of Pepsi...sorry." "It's okay. Don't worry about it."*)

I'm talking about the way that you and I use this catchphrase to simply say *"It's none of your business"* but without the harshness. That's what it means doesn't it? We get an inquiry that we don't want to have to explain so we drop the catchphrase. Some people will utilize it to escape shame and embarrassment as to not get caught. I don't know how you use it, but that simple little catchphrase has been used to fracture so many marriages.

How? **First**, the words *"Don't worry about it"* fractures the sense of oneness of your marriage. Genesis 2:25 (ESV) says, Adam and Eve were "naked and unashamed." There was nothing hidden between them. It's a phenomenal pattern for any marriage. To have emotional, spiritual, mental, and, yes, physical nakedness within your marriage fosters that cohesive oneness that guides a healthy marriage. When you start masking your actions with *"Don't worry about it"*, you are beginning to turn your marriage into two silos instead of the oneness that the Lord intended.

Secondly, the words *"Don't worry about it"* fractures the trust of your marriage. The second you begin to hide actions, thoughts, and feelings behind that catchphrase, you put mystery in the mind of your spouse regarding your "private" life. (NOTE: If you are keeping a private life hidden from your spouse, you've got some serious marital challenges coming your way...but that's for another blog.) I don't care if you don't thing your husband/wife wouldn't understand the business, finances, home, etc. If they're asking about something, tell them. Let him/her decide if they want to ask again.

Ignorance is not bliss! What your spouse needs to see is that your life is an open book to him/her. In 1 Corinthians 7 (ESV), we read "The wife's body does not belong to her alone but also to her husband. In the same way, the husband's body does not belong to him alone but also to his wife." Even though the context is sex and intimacy, the principle of ownership and oneness is applicable. You belong to each other and you cannot purposely keep things whether for convenience, concealment, or solitude.

Lastly, the words *"Don't worry about it"* fractures the your heart toward your spouse. When you start giving yourself permission to use this catchphrase, you are taking one step away from your spouse and one step closer to fostering a heart of a "single" life. When you were not married, you lived and operated for yourself. This can't exist in marriage. But to keep using this catchphrase, you move one step back to that single life. You begin to form a separate life outside of the life of your marriage. Our marriage is echoed out of our relationship with Christ. If we are fracturing our life into a life outside of our relationship with God, it leads to a life of instability. In scripture, James says "Such a person is double-minded and unstable in all they do." Don't invite instability into your marriage or your walk with Christ. Live with the oneness in your heart.

As I stated, "Careful words make for a careful life; careless talk may ruin everything." Guard yourself from this simple catchphrase fracturing your marriage. Talk with your spouse. Ask if he/she has heard you used this one. Ask what they hear when you use it. If needed...ask for forgiveness.

- 38 -

"Spend, don't save"
5 Ways to Invest Time
in Your Marriage

"Oh! Teach us to live well! Teach us to live wisely and well! Psalm 90:12 (MSG)

There are "savers" and "spenders." Judging by the average debt for couples, this country is filled with "spenders." At the same time, looking at a high divorce rate, we have a country of "savers." In other words, we spend money we don't have and misuse the time with our spouse.

Stewardship is really a huge issue in marriage. While I'm not going to turn this into a financial marriage blog, I will turn attention to how much time we spend (or don't spend) upon our marriage.

Please know: You need to work (provision is important). You need alone time (we all do). You need recreation that may or may not include your spouse (I'm not against that). But marriages that are time-starved are adding steroids to issues that have no right exploding to the size they've become. Conflict is inevitable. But when you are depriving your marriage of time, it escalates the size of a molehill into a mountain.

Think about it.

How many misunderstandings could have been avoided by spending time talking to each other in a civilized way?

How many issues are exaggerated because no one has taken the time to talk through things at appropriate moments?

How much assumption is inserted into marriage because nobody thought to take the time to communicate?

How many couples are time-starved because, even though time was spent, it wasn't quality time?

What amounts of stress is being placed upon the marriage because time isn't budgeted properly?

How many couples act like two ships passing in the night because it's been so long since they've planned alone time?

Wrap your mind about what you two are struggling over and ask yourself, "Have we spent quality time together? If we had, could this issue have been avoided?" (Notice I said "quality time" and not just time...there's a difference."

Life is busy. We'll catch up later.

Life is always busy. But in the name of providing, parenting, and even ministry, we've sacrificed time from the one who needs time the most. I love my kids (as they need time too). But what use is it to them for me to deprive my wife of quality time so that we fall apart when they're graduated and gone? What legacy/example to I have my kids if I deprive my spouse

You two need intimacy. And intimacy is essential to a healthy marriage. It doesn't have to cost any money. But it will cost you time. What are you waiting for? Are you "saving" the moments up for a weekend away? Are you waiting for the right moment to give "quality time?" Time is a currency that you cannot save for later. It cannot be saved. You must invest it. And outside of a relationship with Jesus, the best place to invest it is in your spouse.

Here's 5 practical investment tips on time and marriage:

1. **Take the initiative.** Stop waiting for the other person to get motivated. Get out of the childish (and selfish) mindset of "I won't if he/she won't." Put time on the calendar. I do. I block off time for my wife and my family. I block off time for me to be home to get stuff done (sometimes just being home is huge...especially for a quality time-driven person like my wife). Whatever you do, be the one to take the initiative and fight for time together.

2. **Walk through your week together.** Anne and I have a standing appointment every Sunday night. Most of the time, we do it on a walk (good cardio + good communication) but we take a few moments to go over the week. When we do a "flyover" of our week, it gives us a chance to look at our two schedules and talk through what to expect. We both have Google calendars (which are shared so we can see what each other is planning). Those walks help prepare us for our weekly schedule and prevent fights and misunderstandings. It gives us a week-by-week perspective.

3. **Frequent Dates.** You are harshing the buzz of your marriage by not consistently/frequently dating your spouse. It doesn't have to be expensive financially. But investing in intimacy will cost you time. Young in our marriage, dates were as simple as hitting up McDonald's at Midland Mall for an ice-cream cone and walking together. Hit up Redbox and microwave some popcorn. Just pick a time conducive for you two and do something that your spouse wants to do. Just get back to dating and do it frequently.

4. **Maximize moments.** Life is busy all by itself. Add children into the equation, and it's pandemonium. Especially with little ones around and the expense of babysitters, you look for moments to maximize. From going home for lunch during your child's nap to scheduling time when the kids go to bed, find times to develop quality moments with each other. Anne and I used to tape (yes with a VCR) our shows during the week and use specific evenings to make popcorn and enjoy Jack Bauer and Gil Grissom solve criminal activities. Here's another tip: Connect with a few other

families and trade evenings every few weeks where you watch the other family's kids so that you can have a night out.

5. **Rotate between "tastes."** Don't let your definition of quality time be the ONLY definition you work with. Quality time by my definition usually involved two things: Sports and/or sex (why not combine the two?). Anne's definition of quality time doesn't have anything to do with either one of them. She likes shopping, coffee, walking with me, and frozen yogurt (which sometimes gets combined). I work with couples all the time, who have time together, but they feel it's dominated by the preference of one spouse. Trade back and forth on how your time will be spent together.

They say time is our most precious commodity. Whether you realize it or not, it WILL be spent on something. It's up to you to choose what it is being spent upon. Don't wait to spend it on each other when the kids are older. Don't wait till the kids are out of the house. Be liberal with your spending. Splurge your time on your spouse.

Lord, teach us to live wisely and well with our time (Psalm 90:12 NLT).

- 39 -

Passive Aggression...
and it's killing your marriage

Passive aggressive behavior is all about one simple word: disconnect. It's the "disconnect" between what is being said and what is being done. Unfortunately, all around us, marriages are suffering from it. There are many different ways in which passive aggressive behavior can be expressed in our marriage. What I've got written down here is a simple list, though not exhaustive, covers some of the most common examples. I wonder if you can add anything?

1. **Having a hostile attitude.** Passive aggressive spouses tend to assume that something done that they didn't approve of was an intended to be a shot at them. For example, you might assume your spouse know/understands how hard you've been working. When your spouse asks something of you, you assume that he/she has something against you and is trying to use this as a dig against you. It never occurs to you that your spouse simply may not understand the load/pressure that you've been under lately.

2. **The silent treatment.** Nothing highlights disconnect more than the famous silent treatment...and I'm quite skilled at it. There are three common forms:

    o   The Payback: Silence that make you look agreeable but you far from it. You may have lost an argument but this is a pathetic way to get a victory by leaving your spouse in wonderment by making them feel, even though the discussion is over, it's far from over.

o The Cliffhanger: Silence that comes after the word "nothing." "What's wrong?...Nothing" It's just leaves something hanging out there in which you know that there is "something" wrong.

o The Warning Shot: To answer any question with just one word followed by silence. This is intended to signal that there is a problem, without you having to say it.

3. **Building resentment.** Passive aggressive peeps will view requests/demands/issues of others as unfair. Instead of pouring out (expressing their feelings, they'll bottle them up and resent the other person.

4. **Withholding**. In a marriage, it will manifest itself in three ways:

o Withholding intimacy. Instead of the sexual act being a sacred and beautiful moment in a marriage, it's used as a weapon. "Why give my spouse something I know he/she wants? This will teach them to do _____ to me."

o Withholding praise. Some people have a hard time with others, besides themselves, receiving praise. In your mind, it'll keep your spouse humble and/or in the place YOU want them.

o Withholding appreciation. "Nobody thanks me so why do I need to thank him/her." I also like this one, "Why thank her/him for something she/he should already be doing?"

5. **Acts of sabotage.** These are deliberate acts designed to punish your spouse.

o Strategic Procrastination. Consciously putting off what needs to be done. It's usually used as a punishment toward your spouse.

o Intentional mistakes. Rather than saying "no" to your spouse's request, you'll perform the task poorly as to not be asked again.

6. **Manipulative communication.** These will be manifested in:
   o Criticism. A passive aggressive spouse will use a manipulative tongue to criticize but make it appear as a joke or a complement. You may not even catch it till you've left the room or the house.
   o Complaining. Everything in life is a personal attack on them. Anything, and I mean ANYTHING, that doesn't go his/her way is seen as unfair and it an injustice. Every decision is made about him/her because life is all about how it impacts him/her.
   o Sarcasm. It seems that you can't get a straight answer. Sarcastic words are simply indirect put downs to your spouse.
7. **The social media vent.** Instead of facing your spouse, you'll vent over the social media venue of your choice and use it to cut into your spouse. There are usually two reasons for doing this:
   o First, there's something therapeutic about writing something out. I wouldn't discourage journaling or writing your spouse a letter, but social media is public (thus the name).
   o Second, you're most likely using the "venting" to rally your friends/followers to your aid. You're taking it public to get the "public" behind you. You make think it's a good thing, but it really makes you AND your spouse looks bad.
8. **The final blow.** Passive aggressive spouses thrive on getting the last word in. Even if the conflict is over, he/she will slip something in to leave his/her mark on the situation. It may be subtle, but it gives him/her a sense of victory.

You've got to see passive aggression for what it is: Hostility. Like any form of hostility, if you give into it, it will want to rule your life. You and your spouse need to fix the disconnect by doing a few simple things:

1. **Confront the issue by being specific.** Don't dance around it...that's feeding it with more passive aggression.)
2. **Set expectations.** Don't let them be wishy-washy expectations. Use them as boundaries.
3. **Rebuild your communication.** Practice assertiveness and active listening.
4. **Repentance.** Nothing makes a marriage grow more than Christ-like humility.
5. **Pray.** Pray for each other. Pray with each other.

I leave you with Romans 12:18 (NIV), "If it is possible, as far as it depends on you, live at peace with everyone."

- 40 -

"Rearview Mirrors"
3 Simple Steps to Keep Your
Marriage Looking Forward

"...But one thing I do: forgetting what lies behind and straining forward to what lies ahead, I press on toward the goal for the prize of the upward call of God in Christ Jesus." Philippians 3:13-14 (ESV)

Being a dad of a 16-year-old, I have a lot talks about using the car. In fact, I'm trying to get Cammi used to my car instead of Anne's. It's a bit longer and a little more of a challenge to deal with. And if she'll get used to it, it'll prepare her to be a better driver.
But after she backed over my mailbox, I've come to realize we've still got some work to do. She was trying to focus on her rearview mirror and got confused. Even though she was backing up, if she'd just look in front of her, she'd see how straight (or lack-thereof) the car was.

In a car, a windshield is ginormous in comparison to the rearview mirror. The mirror is there to assist you and not be the focal point. What's the focal point? It's this huge piece of safety glass in front of us called a windshield. Our eyes are to be looking forward only to access the mirror for moments of clarity.

The past is a like a rearview mirror: Give it a glance and keep going forward. Too much focus on it has catastrophic results. Unfortunately, too many couples (even singles) struggle with this. You've got a "windshield" to experience the present and move forward into the future. But because of some challenging seasons you've went through, you continue focus upon the past. It's then you get caught up staring and don't realize that living in the past sacrifices the present and mortgages the future.

How do you keep looking forward? It's in the simplicity of what I've been encouraging our congregation to do during our marriage series is:

1. **Encourage Effort.** Encouraging effort keeps your eyes looking forward. Nobody, and I mean NOBODY, should out encourage you when it comes to your spouse. For some reason, we only encourage "successes" and not effort. And what ends up happening is, because "success" is based upon individual's interpretation, encouragement is used very sparingly between couples. From the small moments to the large steps forward, don't wait for results to be encouraging, cheer on the attempts move forward. I'd rather have someone who's failing in their efforts than failing to make ANY effort. Keep looking and moving forward by encouraging your spouse.
2. **Celebrate Progress.** Celebration is largely underestimated. Couples tend to only celibate weightier progress or large steps of progress. But can I present a thought to you? Progress, big or small, is still PROGRESS. When I was doing Weight Watchers 10 years ago, I learned that whether I lost 7 lbs. or 1 oz., it was all progress. And ANY progress is to be celebrated. Progress helps develop momentum. It's that momentum that helps develop the strength to move forward. Want some marriage momentum? big or small, celebrate progress.
3. **Feed Hope.** This is how you keep your eyes looking forward. Hope fixes your focus. Like it or not, if you are not feeding "hope," you're feeding something else. Take your pick, despair, anger, resentment, cynicism, etc. all are bottom feeders that will find sustenance off of hopelessness. My simple, and practical approach: Cut off what is stifling the flames. Push past the feelings of hopelessness and foster an atmosphere of hope. Purpose in your heart that hope is

just as valuable to your marriage as breathing is to your body. And the more you feed hope, the more life you breathe into the lungs of your marriage.

Today, give the past a glance and only a glance. It's there to assist you and not be our focus.

Encourage Effort.
Celebrate Progress.
Feed Hope.

And remember the power of the past is the permission you give it to influence the present!

- 41 -

"Victimizing my Spouse"
4 Reasons Why Sarcasm
Doesn't Work

Words from the mouth of a wise man are gracious, while the lips of a fool consume him ... Ecclesiastes 10:12 (NIV)

I'd say that Anne and I are pretty normal. Do we yell at each other? Yep. Do we fight? Definitely. Do we have moments where feel like terrible parents? Absolutely. Has there been so much frustration that one person had to take a timeout to go for a walk so that further damage wasn't gonna be done during a disagreement? Happened a few months back. But, despite all of this normality, we have a ton of fun together.

In the midst of all of the fun we have, one area we have to constantly watch: sarcasm.

Let me explain.

When we first started dating, the talking was quite innocent and intimate. By "intimate," I mean each conversations opened up another layer of who we were to the other person. Not only did you deliver information, you embraced and digested what was given to you. Whatever was given, you guarded it as a steward over it. Over time, it seems the stewardship can begin to be taken for granted as familiarity breeds contempt. And this is where we get into trouble.

I believe communication is the oil of the engine of marriage. It helps us to continue to be a student of our spouse. But through open communication, we are able to learn new things about our mate that, if we are careless, can be used later for personal humor, or worse, for use when we feel more like adversaries. But the harmful effect of using this knowledge as punch lines or ammunition is significant. Who is going to reveal private and sacred information when it might be used against them?

Anne and I have to confess that there have been times within our own marriage that we've fallen into the trap of zinging each other with sarcasm, claiming that we're "just kidding." And yet later, as we've "talked things out", we better understand the damage it causes. And we've learned there is a difference between sarcasm and being playful:

Sarcasm always has a victim.
Being playful is enjoyed by all.

I can hear some of your thoughts: "We've been doing this for years. We are used to it. It's how we joke." And I understand. Because I've done it. I come from a very sarcastic family who came from a sarcastic lineage. It comes honestly. But your nature (family) and/or how you were nurtured (raised) should never be an excuse for victimizing your spouse with your words. That may sound harsh, but the word "Sarcasm" derives from a word meaning "to tear flesh, like dogs." In essence, it means to be brutal, have no mercy, be vicious, go for the jugular, tear flesh the way a dog would.

Sarcasm victimizes your spouse by...

1. **...clothing, what should be, naked communication.** Love that the book of Genesis describes Adam and Eve as "naked and unashamed." They reached for fig leaves only when shame entered the scene. If you want to reduce the level of intimacy your spouse shares, cause them to want to cover/conceal intimate areas vulnerable to your sarcasm.

2. **...erodes trust.** In the blink of an eye, the security that was the foundation for expression of one's true self can be destroyed. What many couples fail to realize is that an absence of security in communication is like condemning a person to live on an ice-covered sidewalk. Your mate is never truly free to relax because she is continually fighting to keep his/her footing. There's always anxiety that a horrible fall might be right around the corner.

3. **...compromises integrity.** The the rust on the hull of a boat, every barb begins to eat its way through the integrity of the relationship. Intimate knowledge used as punch lines or ammunition causes an internal bruising. Everything about it reduces your spouse's self-confidence as well as their confidence in you.

4. **...preventing personal/marital health.** Sarcasm usually is a smokescreen for things like poor conflict resolution, fear, anger, self-esteem issues, and personal hurt. By not getting help for them, you are cheating both you and your spouse out of a healthy functioning relationship.

Words from the mouth of a wise man are gracious, while the lips of a fool consume him ...(Ecclesiastes 10:12).

If you are done with your marriage being consumed by the "lips of a fool," then it's time for a change.

1. **Be honest with yourselves.** Are you playful or are you sarcastic? Sarcasm is not funny nor is it innocent. It is terribly destructive. Solomon had this to say about the tongue: "The tongue has the power of life and death. Those who love it will eat its fruit." (Proverbs 18:21 NIV) This clearly says that if we plant positive seeds with healthy, loving talk, we will reap its fruit. If we plant weeds of hurtful talk, we will reap that fruit.

2. **Take responsibility for your sarcasm.** You will never change your language unless you take responsibility for hurting your spouse with it. Look carefully and honestly at the impact your language has. Take a fearless inventory of your words. Notice

the ongoing impact of your actions. Notice the lasting damage to your mate's self-esteem. Seek forgiveness. Determine to change.

3. **Make an agreement with your mate to change your language.** Replace indirect, sarcastic insults with clear, respectful, direct messages. Use assertive and edifying language that leads to a healthy connection. Ask for what you want and need in a respectful way. Be quick to listen and slow to speak.

4. **Keep each other accountable for change.** Turning the Titanic doesn't happen in one instance. You may be surprised at how entrenched your behavior patterns are and how difficult it is to change them. However, if you quickly, lovingly, and honestly confront each and every violation, change will occur.

Emotions are contagious. Thus, if you change, it is very likely that your mate will change as well. If you apologize for your sarcastic, biting words, it is likely that your mate will begin changing as well. Loving language and mannerisms encourages loving communication in another.

Do you love your spouse enough to change? Does your commitment to your marriage outweigh the strength of your habits? If so, determine that you will be a playful marriage and not one plagued by sarcasm.

- 42 -

"Sucking The Joy From Your Life!" 10 things I want you to know about comparison

Anne and I have different running styles. The fact is this: We love to run, but there really is nothing similar about the WAY we run.

Anne runs much greater distances but at a slower pace. I run at a much faster pace but at shorter distances. When we run together, the distance she wants to run makes me groan. The pace that I'm used to running frustrates her. When we approach hills, I want to power up them. She likes to walk up them. She can run in the silence of nature and pray and/or reflect upon the day. I love to pray on a run, but I must have something playing in my ears.

Simply said, we approach running quite differently. And neither one is the perfect way to run. We have learned to enjoy our past-time without ruining it with comparing our styles to the other. We've even ceased comparing our running to other people. Anne and I will try to learn more about running, but we've resolved that "comparison" just sucks the joy out of our experience.

Know this: comparison can be a very good thing. From comparing Qdoba to Moe's all the way to comparing running shoes to get the best purchase that gives the best performance. Comparison is a great power that needs to be handled with great responsibility. But unfortunately, it has become a tool for the enemy to use to reduce our joy to dust. I think there might be no other issue that Anne and I counsel more with people than with the issues of comparison. It comes up constantly with us because, as just stated, we hear about it from others and we, Anne and I, can tend to suffer from it. It's brutal and violent. Comparison wants to shred your joy apart to be the shattered remains of what it should be.

As I've said so often to our congregation, *Happiness is a byproduct of circumstantial vision; Joy is a byproduct of Godly perspective.*

What element would love to keep you focused on your circumstances?

Comparison. Like so many things, comparison has been so misused and mishandled that it can be such a detriment to your life. Here are 10 things I want you to beware of when it comes to an unhealthy use of comparison:

1. **Comparison is selfish in nature.** "Why don't I get as much as someone else?"
2. **Comparison is a thief.** It robs the enjoyment from you and others that God designed you to have.
3. **Comparison is used to elevate ourselves instead of God.** "We can do it in order to look better than others."
4. **Comparison can be a cop-out.** We'll find someone who we think is "far worse off", compare ourselves, and give ourselves permission to not change because, "hey, at least I'm not the other person!"
5. **Comparison can be laced with fear.** You match yourself against an ideal and think "I'll never be able to do/accomplish what he/she has done. So why try?"
6. **Comparison is manipulating.** We'll try to use in on our spouse, children, friends, etc. "If I can compare them to who I want, I can steer them in the direction I want them to go."

7. **Comparison is stifling.** We use it to dampen the joy of the people in our life who are celebrating something we can't celebrate with them.

8. **Comparison will make you spiritually impotent.** When you have a reputation of using comparison to stifle joy and manipulate, it can keep you from imparting the love of Christ into others.

9. **Comparison blinds.** It leaves a fog around your life that keeps you unable to see His truth in your life.

10. **Comparison can be judgement.** We can develop an "ideal" and think everyone has to live up to that. People won't know what they want to tell you because they won't know what you're comparing them to.

Be cautious with your living. Watch your life and prevent comparison from sucking the joy out of your walk with Christ. If you're really itching to compare something, then reflect on Psalm 86:8-10 (MSG), There's no one quite like you among the gods, O Lord, and nothing to **compare** with your works. All the nations you made are on their way, ready to give honor to you, O Lord, Ready to put your beauty on display, parading your greatness, And the great things you do— God, you're the one, there's no one but you!

- 43 -

The Bold and the Beautiful: Dealing with Criticism in Marriage

I'll say two things from the "get-go":

1. Criticism can be healthy.
2. Critical people are cancerous.

A relationship that lacks communication, or the wrong kind of communication, is an absolute way for a husband and wife to end up as roommates and not spouses. Communication is one of the most important ingredients in a marriage. I call it the "oil of the marriage engine. Can you imagine going out to lunch with a good friend but saying very little to one another? Better yet, imagine those same two friends doing nothing but criticizing the other—it's hard to imagine, isn't it? Sadly, some marriages are filled with this type of dysfunction; and it's tolerated and it's toxic.

I grew up having a hard time with criticism. I knew I hated it but didn't realize till later in life some of the reasoning's why. One of the biggest contributors is that I am a "words of affirmation" guy. I thrived on encouragement coming from my parents, friends, and authority figures. But just as much as I fed off of edification, criticism broke me down. I wasn't understanding the necessity or the reasoning behind it.

It seemed that friends of mine could take criticism well and even grow off of it yet, for me, it cut me to the bone. For a time, being one of the smallest boys on a large football team had me, on one hand, living with a chip on my shoulder and trying to prove myself and my place on the team. But on the other hand, while watching older and more gifted players getting yelled at, caused me to be paralyzed by fear. If they weren't good enough, what does that mean about me. It wasn't till the breaking point of my senior season, where I discovered that I had been living in a sinking abyss of fear. After a devastating loss, one of our team captains called me out in a team meeting. "If we were as dedicated and practiced as hard as Barringer, we'd be undefeated." I'd have to admit, it might have been the first time I had heard ANY encouragement from a teammate. It shocked me and it changed me. I looked at my teammates, captains, and coaches different. From that point, I not only walked with confidence, but when criticism came my way from the captains or even the coaches, I no longer felt broken down. What made the difference? Two things: First, I understood I was a valuable member of the team. Feelings of insignificance took its toll on me and my play on the field. Second, I caught the heart of teamwork, care, and cooperation behind the team I played with. If I was valuable, then the criticism was actually encouragement. I'll say it this way:

Healthy criticism is never separate from encouragement because they are intertwined. They co-exist. To have one without the other only invites death.

Criticism is sorely misunderstood and misused, especially in marriage. There's such a huge difference between the two statements we started with. But because of the abuse of criticism, the lines are blurred. You have some marriages that desperately need the help that constructive wisdom can help. Without it, spouses keep their marriages on the spinning carousel of confusion and frustration. Yet on the other side, a critical tongue has been used so many times to tear down spouses. I'll give it to you in the form of a TRUTH:

The best way to let your spouse know how deficient they are is to critique everything they do.

It is inevitable in marriages that spouses will, at some point, have things about each other that need to be expressed. Certainly patience, kindness, and humility should be exercised to the greatest degree possible. NOTE: Not every on of your spouse's imperfections or shortcomings needs to be vocalized. However, there are legit moments in which the best course of action for the relationship is to convey a grievance regarding some behavior or issues. Unfortunately, many people approach such discussions in a way that leads to conflict – which exacerbates the problem.

But what I discovered as a member of the Stevenson Titans, is very applicable today. People struggle with criticism in their marriage because:

1. **They don't feel a part of the marriage "team".** Decisions are always one-sided. Feelings are never taken into account. One person enjoys dominating life while the other feels insignificant. Team means you work together. The two become one and act as one. Does your spouse feel like you are a team? Don't answer for them. Ask him/her.
2. **They have never caught the heart of unity, care, and cooperation behind the marriage/team.** With communication breakdown, you really don't know where your spouse's criticism is coming from. If your spouse never hears encouragement/edification from you, your criticism does nothing but break them down with nothing to build upon. I learn that I can't just work out a muscle. I need to eat protein. Working out rips apart the muscle and the protein builds it up to be stronger.

No one really likes to be the object of criticism. No one enjoys having their faults pointed out to them. There is no guarantee that your spouse will respond favorably when approached with a complaint. In fact, it's a natural reaction to respond with some degree of defensiveness. This notwithstanding, if a criticism is presented in a caring, constructive manner, it's very likely the potential of a positive response and outcome are increased.

Here are some ideas to help regarding constructive criticism in your marriage...

(1) **Timing is everything.** Control your tongue (James 1:26 ESV). You have to wait for the right moment. Completely avoid speaking out of frustration or anger. It may feel right to you because you get to fly off at the handle, but in the end it will do more damage. Also avoid initiating the communication at a time or in a location that is not conducive to the conversation (i.e. in front of kids, in-laws, parents, etc). Sometimes a comment is warranted in a moment off need but wisdom needs to be exercised. It's often best to wait for a better time when you are in control of your temper, words, and tones and when the setting provides the best opportunity of your comment being heard.

(2) **Refrain from accusations or attack.** Remember to strive for peace (Hebrews 12:14 ESV). Be cautious to never phrase your criticism in a way that will intentionally invoke a defensive response. Expressing your criticism in the form of nagging or griping will NOT be well received. Name calling or similar tactics are obviously out of the question if you have any hope for a good outcome. My pastor/mentor always taught me: "If the tables were turned, how would I want to be approached?"

(3) **Be assertive, but humble.** Clothe yourself in humility (Colossians 3:12 ESV). There is absolutely nothing wrong with taking the initiative to address a situation in your marriage. If you value your marriage, it is a necessity. It may feel like an undesirable necessity, but it will help avoid future conflict and strife. Deep down, you must have the right intentions, motive, mindset, and attitude. You must get control over your emotions and, above all, approach the task with a sense of humility. Otherwise, your attempts at criticism are doomed for failure and will make matters worse.

(4) **Stand in love.** Love is the only way to walk (Ephesians 5:2 ESV). This means you love, respect and esteem your spouse regardless of faults, mistakes, and so forth. Marriages that are not built on a foundation of the unconditional love of God working through our lives generally will not endure. This has to be expressed and demonstrated consistently in a relationship, even in the midst of conflict, both spouses can feel safe and secure in moving forward.

Conflict is not fun. But it's a part of having two imperfect individuals living in oneness. Keep working as a team and never lose the heart of Christ within your marriage.

- 44 -

"Solving vs. Winning"
4 Tips to Help Solve Marriage Conflict

Anne and I dated for three years (including a year-long engagement). It was a very peaceful dating life. I couldn't tell you about a single fight/disagreement that we had until that one day in Target...

Oh boy.

We were registering for our wedding shower. Target had given us the "scan gun" to document everything we were hoping people would purchase for us. Again, we never worked through conflict because, well, we chose not to fight about anything. But in the "toaster" aisle of the store, Anne found a toaster she wanted. I preferred a different one. Then she said it,
"This is the toaster I want for MY kitchen."

The word "my" set me off like a match to a firework. I lost it. My mind snapped with all sorts of thought followed by words coming out of my mouth,
"Your kitchen? You didn't pay the bills, I do. You don't live there yet, I do. Aren't I going to use the toaster too? Shouldn't I have a say in it?"

This wasn't one of our finer moments (especially for me). I grabbed that scan gun and went after anything that she didn't want me to scan. I scanned PlayStation games. I scanned bottles of Coke. I scanned pretzels. I didn't care. It wasn't about the shower any longer. I wanted to make a point. I wanted to win the argument. After a few choice words, a few tears, and many apologies, we made it through the Target scanning debacle.

It might seem petty to you, but for us at the time (Anne 19, me 22), it was the first time we didn't see eye to eye (that we were willing to admit) and all the pent up frustrations exploded...over a stupid toaster.

(Wedding Shower Tip: Scan your favorite snacks. Everyone who brought us a gift, brought a bottle of Coke and a bag of pretzels. Anne and I cannot exaggerate the literal wall of snacks we were given. Our apartment looked like some huge supermarket display for Coke and pretzels.)

Next month we'll celebrate 18 years of marriage. And of many of the lessons we've learned about conflict, moments like the "toaster moment" have taught us:
"Solving" is better than "winning."

I love Proverbs 16:18 (MSG), "First pride, then the crash - the bigger the ego, the harder the fall."

Pride is the barrier to resolution. Because pride doesn't want to necessarily solve the issue. It wants to win the war. It wants to make a statement. And It feels good to indulge in it. You'll feel like you've got the edge.

But the pride-driven win is never worth the prize. When you see what you've "won," you realize that the pride has caused a crash...destruction. How do you see a win as a "win" when you, through your pride, have reduced your spouse to nothing? As I say so often in counseling, a win for "me" is rarely a win for the "we"; but a win for the "we" is always a win for "me."

My question to you today: Are you looking to win? Or are you looking to solve?

Here's some tips to help. **If you want to be a SOLVER, then...**

1. **Purposely see the good and not the bad.** Why is it so easy to be a critic? I think it has to do with the immediate gain we feel we get. It gives us ammo to use. Pride sees the "bad" as an advantage to have and utilize in case of conflict. A solving spouse looks for the good in the person and actions of their mate. When you search for it, you'll be more apt to act upon it. I think of the words of Paul in Philippians 4:8-9 (MSG), "I'd say you'll do best by filling your minds and meditating on things true, noble, reputable, authentic, compelling, gracious—the best, not the worst; the beautiful, not the ugly; things to praise, not things to curse. Put into practice what you learned from me, what you heard and saw and realized."

2. **Look to grow instead of looking to gain.** Looking to gain against your spouse doesn't help you grow. But looking to grow will help your marriage gain. Solvers are growers. And they know growth necessitates three essential elements: team work and humility. It's that idea of hard-working together and finding ways to grow together instead of trying for personal gain.

3. **Encourage effort over execution.** Far too often, I talk with couples who only hear from their spouse when something is wrong. When I ask about "encouragement," I get people staring at me like I'm talking in the Klingon language (shout out to my Trek friends). Solvers give more than positive reinforcement; solvers build up their spouse. Love what the Hebrew writer exhorts the church to do. "But exhort one another daily, as long as it is called today." Hebrews 3:13 (ESV)

It's more than good church advice. It is great marriage strategy. Catch your spouse doing things right and watch your marriage win. You'll dramatically see the atmosphere of your home completely transform.

4. **Treat your spouse better than he/she deserves.** A solver doesn't treat their spouse like he/she deserves. A solver responds to their spouse like Christ responded to them. When humanity deserved

nothing, Christ gave everything. When everyone pulled back from him, he poured out his love. We people acted in hate to kill him, he offered forgiveness with his final breathes. Solvers recognize that no one in the marriage is perfect. Therefore, our response to each other shouldn't come from a position of who deserves what, but how Jesus love can respond through us.

Pride is so destructive. It'll pervert your mind to the place where you think you can control its power. But pride will manipulate your mind into thinking that winning is what matters. I promise, the way of pride is easier. But cause everything to "crash" (Proverbs 16:18 ESV).

Solving is hard work. Humility will seek to make things right so that it is the Lord and the marriage that shines the most.

"Solving" is better than "winning." Be a solver with your marital conflict.

- 45 -

"Who Need Sex Anyway?"
7 ways to sabotage your
marital sex life

It's always been one of my favorite stories and it was just about the only form of premarital prep that my dad had before marrying my mom. Right before the ceremony, they began to throw a football together. My Uncle David looks at my father and says,
"Harold, how do you think God thinks about sex?"

I'm not sure how dad replied. But Uncle David's reply was priceless, *"God thinks it's great."*

Not sure where we get the idea that anyone, especially Christians, should be silent on the issue of sex. For some reason, we'll shout from the rooftops all of the blessings that God has given us but we stay strangely silent on the issue. But with our (the church) silence, I believe, we've seen a toll taken upon our world. We can blame Hollywood or any type of media outlet. I'm of the opinion that we (the church) stayed silent over something God wasn't silent about. Since no one stepped up to the mic, someone else did. And now we are playing catch-up with a deranged understanding of this awesome and amazing gift given to our marriage by God himself.

My heart behind today's blog is to help bring liberty and freedom to married couples. Again, sex is a gift from God. Like any gift from God,

Satan would love to pervert the truth as to change it into the image that he desires. In fact the definition of the word "pervert" is, "alter (something) from its original course, meaning, or state to a distortion or corruption of what was first intended." And that's exactly what he's accomplishing.

God desires you to have a prosperous sex life in your marriage, yet there are some things we do to sabotage the enjoyment. Like everything from God, we are called to be stewards. And yes, you are to be a steward of your sex life as to not damage this blessing.

Here we go, **7 ways to sabotage your sex life:**

1. **Use guilt.** Manipulating the emotions of your spouse might win you a battle or two but you'll lose the war. Using guilt is wrong and abusive and it'll make your spouse despise every act that is supposed to bring your marriage joy. I've always taught: God uses conviction; Satan uses guilt. Conviction is a job of the Holy Spirit to prod us to move forward. Guilt, by design, wants to keep us in a place of blame. You're not the Holy Spirit so stop trying to convict your spouse and/or stop acting like Satan and guilting your spouse. Guilt is not your role.
2. **Wait till you are in the mood.** Sex not a gift just for the spouse with the higher libido. It is a gift from God for you both. Imagine with me, your love language is "Quality Time" and your spouse responds to that need with "I'm not in the mood." Or maybe you're a "Words of Affirmation" person and desire conversational intimacy but what you get is "No thanks, I don't feel like that today." In the words of my amazingly wise wife, you are the only one in this world that can sexually satisfy your spouse. Regardless of what your love language is, we are called to serve our spouse (not just sexually). Be open and be creative. Take some steps forward, not out of guilt or condemnation, but out of a genuine heart to fill your spouse's "love tank" to FULL. If your marriage is made up of two people desiring to serve each other (pouring into your spouse's needs), the two of you will never run on EMPTY.

3. **Invite pornography into your marriage.** This is not just a male issue. Both men and women can be stimulated by pornography and seduced into thinking it's a help for their marriage. The goal of pornography is to skew the authentic with fantasy. Whether its "Visual" or "Emotional" porn, it is a huge stumbling block for couples and causes tremendous sexual issues. Two of my biggest reasons is it causes an unhealthy view of the female body as well as unhealthy sexual expectations. Top it off with the addictive nature of porn devised to make you dependent upon it, you then have a monster that isn't worth the amount of space it will take up in your thoughts. Like a thirsty man crawling through the desert after a mirage, pornography has you crawling toward an illusion that will leave you constantly in want.

4. **Comparison with other couples.** We all get caught doing it. We listen to another couples and/or see their marriage lived out on social media. Comparison can be dangerous because it either puts us in a place of condemnation or competition with/by other couples...both of which are extremely unhealthy in marriage. Just as you are uniquely made by God, the two of you as a couple are unique in your oneness. Simply said, you two are not called to do and act like other couples when it comes to their marriage practices. Yes, there will be characteristics we all possess as we strive to have our marriages reflect Christ. But the manner and frequency will differ based upon the two people who make up the marriage. When it comes to the frequency of sex, there is no magic number. Assuming someone else has a BETTER quality sex life because they have more quantity isn't a healthy mindset (not that I'm against quantity). But comparison will break you down and take your satisfaction from your spouse and place it upon the opinions of others.

5. **Make intimacy all about intercourse.** Intimacy is the culmination of a day and not just a few moments in a bedroom. Sex is bigger than intercourse. It's bigger than foreplay. It encapsulates the way you text, call, serve, respond, and look at each other throughout the day. A great way to sabotage your sex life is to think that what

takes place between the sheets is completely disconnected from the rest of life. Open your eyes. Perhaps he/she is struggling to respond to you because you haven't responded to him/her all day.

6. **Stop having fun together.** You can't discount fun in a marriage. Dates cannot be rare occasions. Anne and I, early in our marriage, didn't have much money or ability to just leave the house because of two little ones. It didn't stop us from enjoying time with each other. From projects and walks together to watching shows on our laptop, we found ways to engage in "fun" things that we both enjoy doing together. Laughing together is good for the heart, good for the soul, and can stir the libido. Fun is mandatory inside and outside of the bedroom. Learn to enjoy each other.

7. **Ignore past hurts.** It's painful to remove a splinter in your hand. What's even more painful is to wait thinking it'll go away. The longer you wait, the deeper the actual wound will get. First, if you have past sexual hurts that you have carried into your marriage, tell your spouse and let him/her help you. Remember, the two became one. What is your issues is his/her issue and you move forward together. Second, please get some help ASAP. You've held onto it long enough and that hurt has no right in your life. Find a local Christian counselor that specializes in this and begin the road to healing. The healing that comes from the atonement of the cross includes our deepest hurts.

I end with this…Proverbs 5:18-19 (TLB), "Let your manhood be a blessing; rejoice in the wife of your youth. Let her charms and tender embrace satisfy you. Let her love alone FILL you with delight."

A key word (amongst many keywords) in this passage is "FILL." Just as much as sex is a gift from God, you are a gift to your spouse. You are the ONLY ONE that is equipped to "FILL" your spouse with "delight." If you are in a place of hurt or confusion, please seek Godly help. Don't wait on it. I've never met a couple that had a healthy sex life that got divorced. I think the biggest reason behind that is they've learned to serve each other by "delighting" their spouse. And if your spouse is full, there is no room for Satan to work with.

- 46 -

"The lingerie of life."

Lingerie is meant for one thing: attraction...

...and the attraction it was designed for is meant to lead to intimacy.

Anne will say, it doesn't take much to attract me to her. It could be the "typical man" type of mindset, but I began to ask myself the other side of that: what repels me? What turns me off? What spoils the beauty of an individual?

What I feel the Lord dropped in my heart was so simple.

Your words.

I looked at Anne this morning said, "I've got it. Words are 'the lingerie of life.'" She looked a bit confused and slightly concerned over my mental state. I went on to explain, when our words are poured out to our spouses, it can make us to most appealing, attractive individual. It becomes a "turn on" to our spouse. I'm not saying there's immediate sexual desire that stirs. But there is an emotional intimacy that connects to our spouse's heart that draws them to you.

I have been thinking about attacking the issue of our words. While mulling this blog over, it was just a few days ago when a friend, that is passionate about marriage, sent out the tweet:

"Make love with your words outside the bedroom. That really helps during love-making in the bedroom."

It was confirmation of what I wanted to deal with today. We need to have marriages that will foster love and intimacy with their words. They need to see their communication (verbal and nonverbal) are more intertwined with the bedroom than they thought.

Have you ever met someone who became the most unattractive and unappealing person by their words? I recall my single life when I would see a young lady that, outwardly, was attractive to me only to be turned off by what came out of her mouth. To put the shoe on the other foot, I wonder how many times I repelled a young lady away by some of the words/phrases I used. Our words are more powerful than what we give them credit for.

It becomes a confusing state. In our minds, the other person is surface attractive...BUT something about their words (tones, mannerisms, phrases, character issues) is transforming them before our eyes into something that repels us away. It is truly unfolding what the scripture says in Matthew 12:34 (ESV), "For out of the abundance of the heart the mouth speaks." Our words bring to fruition what lie beneath our surface. I heard, years ago, that sex begins in the kitchen (actually, it's a best-selling book). I'm not talking about locations for you and your spouse to make love. I'm talking about how intimacy begins from the moment you wake up. Why the kitchen? That's where people are, on the most part, fully awake having breakfast. I'll admit, Anne and I don't talk much in the morning till we are fully awake. It's like a scene from "The Walking Dead" where two zombies are wandering till showers and caffeine kick in. But when we do begin to talk...that's where our intimacy begins. Again, couples, especially men, have to get out of their minds that intimacy is when the lights turn off and you are under the covers.

There is so much dysfunction in marriages when it comes to attraction. On one hand, you've got on spouse who can be turned on at a moment's notice regardless of the day or time. On the other hand, the other is in no mood because the "abundance of the heart" of their spouse has been on display all day and has made that him the most unappealing individual. Once we close the door, we assume it's time for intimacy. Most don't realize, if that's when you're ready to foster intimacy, you are a number of hours too late.

I believe that you and I can foster and atmosphere of intimacy and attractiveness in our marriage by having naked conversations. Before you freak out and I now become your husband's favorite pastor by encouraging nudity, I'll explain what I mean. Genesis 2:25 (ESV) says Adam and Eve were "naked and unashamed." There, consistently, was nothing hidden in their marriage. Everything about them was open to see. Put your defenses down and have consistent, open, and honest communication. By raising up conversational walls/barriers between you and your spouse, you will cover the openness/nakedness that your marriage was meant to have. I'll give you a TRUTH:

Without talking, your marriage will not survive. The more you openly communicate, the closer you will be.

Here's some helpful tips:

1. **Timing is everything.** When you reconnect with your spouse at the end of a workday, don't launch into your frustrating day immediately. Intimacy is just like good comedy...it's all about timing. Let the moments create conversational opportunities and flow.

2. **Do some spouse reconnaissance.** Reconnaissance is a mission to obtain information by visual observation or other detection methods. Find out what humor's your spouse and look for ways to insert humor into your conversations. What do they like to talk about? What do they see as fun? Don't have your conversations be "all business" (kids, finances, mother-in-law, etc). When Anne knows there's a significant game on tv, she'll ask about it even

though she doesn't care about sports. She cares because I care. It means the world to me.

3. **Provide emotional support, validation, and compliments.** If you don't feel that you spouse likes and respects you, there will not be a strong connection. You have to lift each other up and let each other know the depth of your caring. He/she needs to know you care. How do emotional affairs start? When someone at home ceases to care and opens up the job to someone else to care. Don't be that husband/wife who does that!!! No one will should out-compliment me when it comes to Anne. No one should beat me as her biggest supporter.

4. **Don't be afraid to get "dirty"...but be careful.** Being great roommates just won't cut it. There has to be the desire to be together as a couple. Sensuality is a great part of a healthy marriage. I use the word "dirty" but there's nothing wrong/dirty about it. The desire you have for sensuality is God-given. He designed you that way. But remember: there's a time and place. At the dinner table in front of the kids? Unless you want them to go into counseling... please save it for a more appropriate time. You may think the spark has gone, but there are too many ways conversationally to rekindle it. Send messages (please be careful) to your spouse. It'll make them come home earlier than expected. Make your spouse feel like the most attractive person alive. Let him/her know you still desire them. All you have to do is try.

5. **Be humble...always.** Express Compassion, repentance, acceptance, and forgiveness. Humility will show you the way through difficult seasons. Humility is sexy. As your marriage grows, there will be losses, challenges, and some things that you just can't fix in your own power. Dealing with the storms together is a big part of what relationships are all about. We all mess up. Learning to understand and let go of mistakes that you or your spouse make will turn your life around and foster more time for joy.

6. **Pray together.** It doesn't have to be a prayer that recaps the entire Pentateuch. Keep it simple. Create moments when there is conversational intimacy that involves you, your spouse, and the

Lord. He established the institution of marriage. It's only right to keep him in our conversational intimacy. Spiritual intimacy becomes the fuel for deeper emotional and physical intimacy. It reconnects you to the One you were designed to be in fellowship with and opens up depths to the rest of our oneness with our spouse.

Keep growing your intimacy. Keep up the pursuit of your spouse. Don't forget the lingerie (referring to this article).

- 47 -

"Unsubscribe"
6 things you should
unsubscribe from your life

I'm in a mode right now. I have been cleaning up my email life by "unsubscribing" from all kinds of stuff. Restaurants, retailers, and random businesses are the latest victims to my shedding off of my email weight. It's not that I am boycotting them. I'm just done.

This is going to sound petty, I'm tired of hearing notifications throughout the day that distract me for no good reason. I wasn't even reading them anymore. I was just tolerating them, discarding their info, and yet doing absolutely nothing about it.

I'm taking back my email (even though most people don't use it... most of my interaction takes place over social media). I'm done with superfluous crap that takes up time, attention, and screen space.

So many of us are tolerant of ridiculous situations in our life that have claimed to much time, attention, and well, space in your life. Like my ridiculous metaphor, I'm not asking you to boycott people per se. I'm not asking you to unfriend/unfollow them (even though that's necessary sometimes), but it's time to develop healthy boundaries in your life. Proper boundaries aid you in keeping out unhealthy influences. They are about taking responsibility for our own lives. Your marriage needs healthy boundaries. Your kids need them. Your personal life needs them. Boundaries are necessary for a self-controlled, God-honoring life. And sometimes those boundaries are the necessary means to cut off the intimate connection to things/people who have no desire to help you but tear you down.

James 2:1 (MSG) "My dear friends, don't let public opinion influence how you live out our glorious, Christ-originated faith."

I want you to cut the umbilical cord that these things/people have been using to feed off of your joy. Scripture says "The joy of the Lord is my strength." The goal of these things/people is to control you! It's time to keep your joy and say goodbye to the stuff you don't need.

Today is your day to unsubscribe to these 6 types of people:

1. **The Critical.** Aggressive and deadly. These things/people have something to say about everything and cannot be happy for anyone else. Unless the idea and/or solution came from them, it's not worth entertaining. These type of people have something crass to say about everything...even if it's a little jab. They cannot help but be critical.

2. **The Discouragement.** From people, to news outlets, discouragement is everywhere. Sometimes it's not as aggressive as the critical. Discouragement's M.O. tends to be a slow death to your joy. It constantly whittles away at your joy. Think of having a full pool. The more you entertain discouragement in your life, the more it is emptying the pool out till you have nothing left but a hole in the ground. An empty pool is purposeless. And that's what a lifestyle of entertaining discouragement feels like...purposeless.

3. **The Drama.** People with drama issues love company. Why? Without the company of others, it's just a one-person show. And, usually, that's a tough thing to pull off. Drama sucks you in to not just a story-line, but desires you to take on a role. To entertain drama in your life is like attending a casting call and you are the director's favorite choice for the part. Back away. Let the curtains close. This part is not for you.

4. **The Campaigner.** Call them gossips and/or slanderers. This is a close cousin to "drama." The difference is, these are people who

don't necessarily want to pull you into the drama. It's just they can't keep their mouth shut about information they've come across. Like having poison ivy, they're trying to itch what they have whilst spreading it around. It feels good to get info. In fact, you feel powerful. But in the end, you wind up realizing what you possess not only poisons your mind, it poisons your relationships.

5. **The Instigator.** They know what button to press. They know when to press it. Like Buddy the Elf in the elevator of the Empire State Building, The Instigator wants to press as many buttons in your life and then step away while you sit in your hurt, anger, frustration, and/or embarrassment. These people want to start a fire without the responsibility of dealing with the fire. They are relational arsonists. Smokey the Bear says "only you can prevent forest fires." I'd say, "Only you can prevent the spread of relational fires."

6. **The One-Upper.** The "One-Upper" will never let you be in a place of joy because what you have doesn't compare to what they possess. You can't share celebration points, success stories, and/or the blessings God has given to this person. Why? Because they're prepared to squash it. He/she cannot handle letting someone have something he/she doesn't possess. The catastrophic results to your life is the more your joy is stifled, the more apt that your joy will be completely blown out.

I'm not asking you to stop influencing people like these 6. Like you and me, they are candidates of the redemptive power of Christ. Like you and me they're imperfect and need to see the continual work of the Holy Spirit to help them every single day. But it's time to unsubscribe to their influence. It's time to stop giving them the time, attention, and space in your life. As I said before, I want you to cut the umbilical cord that these things/people have been using to feed off of your joy. Why? Because what influences affects "how you live out our glorious, Christ-originated faith."

It's time to unsubscribe. It's time to take back your life.

- 48 -

"Stupid Spouse"
A culture of demeaning our mate

I do like sitcoms (situational comedies). I grew up watching them. You probably have your favorites. I've got mine (MASH, Newhart, Taxi, Cosby Show, and Home Improvement). The really good sitcoms take everyday situations for the everyday person and makes them funny. It's what keeps our attention and helps us to see the humor in own lives. Now that Netflix has "Everyone Loves Raymond," I find myself finally watching the show right before I sleep just to let the comedy relax my mind before sleep.

But...it's got me thinking.

At 30-minute intervals, we see situations revealed and the comedy unfold. While we watch, we, and especially our children, subliminally soak in messages and quotes. They sit in our minds and crowd up our memories. (Even now, you're thinking of your own favorite sitcoms and/ or the quotes and moments that stick out to you.) Unfortunately, over the years, there seems to be a steady vein running through most sitcoms. It was there from my earliest memories of seeing "The Honeymooners" and it lingers now into our modern-day shows.
The "Stupid Spouse."

stu·pid/ˈst(y)o͞opid/ lacking intelligence or common sense.

Most of you reading this won't have to think back very far to see the sitcom with the "Stupid Spouse." You name the sitcom and you'll have no problem naming off the spouse or the person in the relationship that has been chosen to be "stupid." Not only is he/she the butt of the jokes, but the role that he/she plays becomes a laughing-stock of their family. Children are allowed to disregard dad because he's an idiot. Don't respect mom because she's disconnected from reality. Husbands are spineless and weak leaders. Wives are selfish and conniving. There is very little respect for marriage as well as parenting.

My wondering: has what we have been viewing and enjoying been allowed to soak into our own families? Have we allowed our entertainment to actually shape our marriages? Have they become emotional pornography creating unrealistic ideals that ravage the reality of how the Lord has designed you both? Do you have a culture of demeaning your spouse?

Our homes SHOULD be the place of safety. Our spouse SHOULD be our greatest supporter. Our marriage SHOULD be the source of our greatest encouragement.
But somewhere in this demeaning culture, we have become what we watch. We tear down our spouse. Now we don't do it to their face all the time. Let them leave the room first before we give a comment to our kids about how you disagree with their father/mother. When our parents call us, we'll start-up again on how "stupid" our spouse is. We'll even go to church and sing of the love of God and put on the facade to our friends of how our family is. Somewhere this has to stop. Someone has to draw a line in the sand and make a stand for encouragement.

James deals this sensitive subject by saying, "From the same mouth come blessing and cursing. My brothers, these things ought not to be so."

If you find yourself thinking about how stupid (lacking intelligence or common sense) your spouse is...

If you are constantly refusing to let your spouse be a helpmate...
If you cannot speak to them respectfully and lovingly...
If you cannot talk about your spouse without tearing them down to someone...
Husbands and wives...THESE THINGS OUGHT NOT TO BE SO!

Before you cancel your cable, Netflix, and Hulu accounts, take a step back. I'm not telling you to go all "Pharisee" on me with your TV's and computers. I'm asking for you to just pause and reflect. It's time to turn the tide of the culture of your home.

1. **It starts with you.** I've dealt with too many marriages where a husband and wife are acting like middle schoolers and not adults. Don't wait for him/her to make the first move to having a culture of respect and honor. Thank the Lord that Jesus didn't wait for us to make the first move back to him before he extended love toward us. "Drawing a line in the sand" ISN'T about "do this or I'm leaving." It's about saying, "It stops here and now." STOP TRYING TO CHANGE YOUR SPOUSE! Let the change start in you.

2. **Ask for forgiveness.** Admitting fault is not a sign of weakness. It's a sign of strength. Hiding your faults is what makes you weak. Humility is the antibiotic for a pride-filled marital culture. Proverbs 22:4 says, "The reward for humility and fear of the Lord is riches and honor and life."

3. **Create culture.** Embrace who your spouse is and how the Lord created them as an individual. Your differences are to be celebrated... not rejected. Create a culture where encouragement and praise becomes the norm. When there is a culture of edification, the constructive criticism that is needed for growth is received on furtive soil as opposed to calloused hearts that have been damaged by harsh remarks and disrespect. You may have been married 2 years, 20 years, or 40 years. It's not too late to create a new culture of encouragement that will foster the atmosphere of healthy marital growth.

4. **Lastly, be dedicated to feeding the new culture.** Occasionally, Anne ticks me off. I never make her mad (okay that's a lie). But there needs to be a decision that, no matter how out of the norm it is for you, to feed the culture of encouragement and honor. Your kids cannot see and hear you demeaning their father/mother. Your parents cannot hear you tearing your spouse down. Before other and before the Lord, chose to be a spouse who builds instead of destroys. Ephesians 4:29 (NLT) says, "Don't use foul or abusive language. Let everything you say be good and helpful, so that your words will be an encouragement to those who hear them." You will have moments that you will not feel like feeding the "new culture." That's where we come to grips with the fact that love is a decision and not just a feeling. Love your spouse to feed the culture of a healthy marriage.

If we were real here, we'd admit we ALL have moments where we are lacking intelligence or common sense. Be humble to see that in yourself and that humility will feed into how you deal with your spouse.

Encourage liberally. Laugh loudly. Love unconditionally.

- 49 -

"Under-appreciated"
Building a Culture of Appreciation

I got a text from Anne the other day. She's been getting in the habit of dreaming/thinking about marriage blogs during her running times (I'm beginning to rub off on her). She's begun to make a list of needed topics for our weekly marriage blog. Today was first on her list.

It amazing me how often this subject comes up. Whether it's someone talking about their job, their volunteer work, or a sensation in their family, there are so many people feeling under-appreciated. Of all places, marriage shouldn't be one of those places.
When it comes to marriage, both husbands and wives should be thankful and appreciative of their spouse. But I feel it should be more often. I added the "more often" because I'm willing to bet that most of you reading this are already appreciative of your spouse. Like me, perhaps there's also room for improvement. About a month and a half ago, I preached a message on "encouragement" and I feel I can't get that message out enough. And I believe part of "encouragement" is showing appreciation.

My question for you today: Are you building a culture of appreciation.

Here's what I mean.

I'll admit that I'm not always appreciative of Anne...at least not as much as I could be.

For example:

- There are days when I tell her how much I appreciate her. These are our "cheesy" moments!
- There are days when I appreciate the things Anne does to make my life easier…but I just don't tell her that. I'm not sure why. I figure she already knows how I feel anyways.
- There are days when Anne's less than desirable qualities overshadow her desirable qualities and I am clearly NOT appreciative of anything at that moment.

I know I should be doing more of the first statement, But I don't. Why? Well, the reasons vary. I may be tired. I may be grouchy. I could be too stubborn because I want to be complemented first. Anne may be in a bad mood. We may have gotten into an "disagreement". I may just not feel like it because of all of the aforementioned reasons. In other words, I'm human; I act less than an ideal at times. Not a cop-out, just a fact. How do we make our spouse feel under-appreciated?

1. **Take for granted what they do.** It seems like after the "honeymoon" phase of life, we stop noticing what our spouse does. Whether their job, things around the house, or stuff that involves the kids, stop noticing how hard they work.
2. **Feel entitled to the little things.** Entitlement give you a superiority complex with your spouse. And that doesn't feed the oneness of the marriage. It rips it apart. "I'm entitled to _____…she/he's my spouse! I shouldn't have to ask for _____" Guard yourself from entitlement.
3. **Make sure you deserve more.** This is where you see that your spouse has had a rough day but, you build up your day as to say, "you think you had it bad, you didn't have to deal with what I did today." Not only have you missed the opportunity to pour healing into your mate, you've selfishly diverted any appreciation and encouragement that was needed for them back onto you. I'm not keeping you from feeling appreciated. BUT some people

struggle with other people being blessed besides themselves. Be other-centered.

4. **Criticism.** Some people, I think, don't really hear how pessimistic they are. Maybe they don't realize that criticism is the first thing to come out of their mouth. "We'll I don't want them to get a big head", or "I don't want their hopes to build up" or even better, "I'm just keeping it real." I'll give ya a TRUTH: Criticism without encouragement isn't help. It's abuse. Let the Holy Spirit do the job of keeping them humble.

Ephesians 4:29 (NIV) "Let no unwholesome word proceed from your mouth, but only such a word as is good for edification according to the need of the moment, that it may give grace to those who hear." That word "edification" means the act of promoting other's growth. With your words and actions of appreciation, you are literally building them up and promoting growth in their life.

I want to give you another TRUTH: Everyone needs to feel appreciated. In your marriage, this is so, so extremely vital. When one spouse feels under-appreciated, things go awry. And the crazy thing is, you may not even realize this until they mention it. I don't always realize I'm like this until Anne and I have both alluded to the fact that we didn't feel appreciated by the other for one reason or another. At this point, whoever was the listener goes into "damage control" and offers a "token appreciation." The problem is I don't like the idea of responding after-the-fact to things. I'd rather be proactive in every area of my life (or at least I do my best to be proactive). And proactive means telling my wife how appreciative I am of her so she doesn't think otherwise (and vice versa). Citing examples of what specifically she does — the little things or the big things — is even better. (It shows I'm not just parroting empty marriage advice.) It's funny too, to see my husband's reaction when I do tell him how much I appreciate him, because it catches him off guard at first but then he appreciates me for saying it. It's a nice feeling.

Some ways to express appreciation:

1. **Speak appreciation; communicate it so they can hear it.** Most of you know what language your spouse hears. Is it physical touch? Is it words of affirmation? Gifts? Whatever language they speak, express appreciation back to them. Cite examples. List them out. This tells them (1) you cared enough to notice something and (2) you cared enough to give appreciation in a language he/she understands.

2. **Plan out appreciation.** Get a babysitter and plan an evening out together as pure appreciation for your spouse. Better yet, plan a weekend away WITHOUT kids. Make the plans about what your spouse would enjoy the most. Appreciation is where the line "it's the thought that counts" really rings true. It doesn't have to be an expensive plan. Just the fact that there is a plan carried out and expressed will do so much.

3. **Live out appreciation; make it a daily habit!** Be proactive with appreciation in your marriage! Tell them how much you appreciate them daily. Don't give a token "thank you" but specifically cite examples. "I really appreciate when you do _____", or even, "Thanks for doing _____. I really appreciate it!" By doing so, you ensure you have a spouse who feels appreciated and who more than likely, will reveal their appreciation of you in return.

Remember this last TRUTH: An appreciated spouse always makes for a happier spouse!

- 50 -

"Just like the picture": 4 Approaches to Developing the Uniqueness of Your Marriage

---

Thank you for making me so wonderfully complex! Your workmanship is marvelous--how well I know it." Psalm 139:14 (NLT)

As a pastor, I tend to visit the same places in my city. Admittingly, I'm a creature of habit but this goes deeper than that.

I visit the same coffeehouse every day. I go to the same chicken place on Wednesdays. I get my haircut at the same location by the same person every other week. Familiarity and frequency helps me to develop connection with people in the community. It helps me develop relationships and moves conversations past "weather talk" into deeper things (this would make a great blog idea for pastors).

Last week, I had a conversation with the young lady who cuts my hair. Amidst talking about her family and the salon she manages, a statement about she only likes to cut guy's hair. When I enquired why that was, she talked about her frustration with ladies who are excited about an image clipped out of a magazine of a someone's hair and demand that be done to them. More often than not, they'll leave upset that the result doesn't "look like the picture." She says that people don't get the number of components that are in play with the hairstyles they covet. The type of hair, shape of head, how well they take care of their hair, etc.

In other words, customers were demanding the picture-perfect results but don't account for the factors at play.

That conversation got me thinking about how that translates to marriage. Quite often, I meet couples who take for granted the UNIQUENESS of their marriage (heck, I still do it). We chase the picture of perfection that we see in someone else and want to get there without the hard work of dealing with the individual factors you both bring. While we all understand that we married someone quite different from ourselves, we still get frustrated. But I'm afraid many assume your individual differences compound your marital problems instead of seeing how they add into your uniqueness. Your perspective of how you perceive your differences changes the scope of your marital health.

I love what the Psalmist says, "Thank you for making me so wonderfully complex! Your workmanship is marvelous--how well I know it." Psalm 139:14 (NLT)

If we believe in the "oneness" of marriage, can we not look at our marriage in the same light as the Psalmist looked at individual lives? Your marriage is "wonderfully complex" and the "workmanship is marvelous." And I wonder if the first step to embracing the wonderful complexity of marriage is to accept what makes you both distinct. Differences are a good thing; they're not automatically an impairment. Just because our spouse and marriage are different doesn't mean it's wrong. It means we have a unique marriage and bring unique individual qualities to the marriage.

Simply said: Stop trying to achieve an image. Build your marriage from the inside out.
Finding uniqueness means that marriage will never look "just like the picture" of some else's marriage. Don't cookie-cutter yourselves. You

may seek health, but EVERY couple works with different factors that are peculiar to your marriage. Consider...

- Your backgrounds.
- Your personalities.
- Your likes and dislikes.
- **Your skill-sets.**

How do you develop the uniqueness of your marriage?

1. **Look at the reality.** No one is perfect, and therefore, there is no perfect marriage. So, my recommendation is to stop seeing perfection in others and stop expecting it in your spouse and/or marriage. The only things to expect in yourself and your spouse is humility, teamwork, and growth. In my opinion, there are only two types of marriages: Those who work on them and those who don't. Be the first type.

2. **Learn to appreciate your spouse.** Vision is everything. The direction of your marriage will go in the direction of your focus. And if you learn to look for the good in your spouse, your marriage will go in that direction. Differences do not automatically mean "wrong," many times, they simply mean "different." And when you bring value to those differences, you bring value to your spouse.

3. **Learn how to express appreciation.** Silent appreciation is not appreciation at all. Let me take that a bit deeper: appreciation with strings attached is not appreciation at all. Gratitude has the ability of elevating our attitudes above bitterness. Let it be said of your home that, while you don't have marital health figured out, you do have an atmosphere of which health can grow. And that atmosphere is "appreciation/gratitude." A rule that I try to enforce with my family (as well as my staff): For every negative thing, be sure to bring up two to three positives. The simplicity of the exercise will help retrain your negative mind into a more positive one.

4. **Pray for blessings on your spouse and ask the Holy Spirit to bring change in you.** Sometimes we can spend too much energy trying to do the work of the Holy Spirit instead of releasing Him to bring the change only He can bring. I think we can transform our attitudes by first praying for blessing upon our spouse and then allowing the needed change in our marriage to BEGIN with ourselves. Humility in the heart paves the way for the formation of healing and health.

When it boils down to it, the more you follow a "perfect image" of a marriage that you've seen on social media or in someone you know, the more you'll wind up frustrated in your marriage. The more you follow a Perfect Savior, the more you'll see your imperfections and see an opportunity for His grace to shine through your marriage. The two of you, as a unit, are "wonderfully complex" and His "workmanship is marvelous." Today...

Be the blessing your marriage needs.
Be the change your marriage needs.
Love your spouse through the love you've received from Christ.

- 51 -

"What I learned from my parent's 42 years of marriage"

in 2015, my parents celebrated their 42nd anniversary. I often get asked about when my passion for marriage began. It began with my parents, Hal and Linda. Watching their marriage not only made me want what they had, but shaped the marriage I have. Don't get me wrong, as they'll tell you, they are by no means the model of perfection (ever seen my dad BBQ in shorts, black socks, and dress shoes after church?), but their ability to stay humble and keep Christ at their center for 42 years is astounding.

Of the plethora of lessons, I've learned from them, parenting has been a major theme they've mentored me in. Here's one lesson they've taught me for every year they've been married.

1. Jesus is our true north. Our family centers upon him.
2. Sometimes your just your presence will speak louder than anything. (They never missed a football game)
3. Effort is always rewarded above accomplishment.
4. Love was never earned.
5. Michigan NOT Michigan State football.
6. You can't love your children the same. You may love them the same *amount* but you show it different because they are *different*!
7. Somehow, when the grandkids showed up, I've taken a backseat to them.

8. Every moment can be a teachable moment.
9. Mom and dad NEVER sought to be my best friend. (I had enough friends...I needed parents.)
10. You can survive ANYTHING. (Their handling of the most devastating moment a parent could ever experience has profoundly changed me and countless others.)
11. Apologizing to your children for your human mistakes will make you a hero.
12. Homes should be a source of laughter.
13. Be in the Word. (Worn out bibles were a common sight in the house.)
14. Church isn't optional for us as a family. (When the doors were opened, Kid's Church or not, we were there.)
15. Hard work is important to develop at the youngest of ages.
16. It's impossible to say "I'm proud of you" enough to your kids.
17. Having a reputation of being the only dad who'll QB for the neighborhood kid's football game is a cool thing to have.
18. Serving your church community is what you do. Be the first to volunteer.
19. Don't be naive about your children. (The words "my kid would never do that" didn't come from their mouth. Because Rachael and I are human, they always knew we were capable of doing wrong.)
20. Forgiveness is liberating.
21. Your kids need to hear you pray over them in locations other than the dinner table.
22. Tithing wasn't optional. My first 10% belonged to Jesus.
23. Lying can get your mouth washed out with soap.
24. I can never give them too many grandkids.
25. Dad's first ministry was to his wife.
26. Sickness demanded prayer and anointing oil (from dad's key chain).
27. Trying to steal a taste of turkey while dad is carving it without getting stabbed is a part of Thanksgiving.
28. Phone calls with mom rarely end without an "I love you."

29. The only future that mattered was that I was serving the Lord. (My vocation mattered less than my direction.)
30. I'm not psychologically damaged because I was spanked. (If I had a "timeout," it was after I was spanked.)
31. Mom had more grace with report cards. (It's why dad made the rule that report cards came to him first.)
32. Giving to missions wasn't optional.
33. They grew their marriage to outlast the kid's time in the home.
34. No human being exists that can out encourage mom and dad.
35. Dedication in the dictionary says, "See Hal and Linda Barringer."
36. Kids need to see their parents show affection to each other (verbal and physical).
37. Kids need to receive affection from their parents (verbal and physical).
38. Dad always stood in defense of mom to us. (Talking back to her was never tolerated.)
39. Humility means we step back and let God take the curtain call.
40. Don't wait till tomorrow to spend time with your children.
41. Crowns and accolades belong at the feet of Jesus.
42. Live out a Romans 8 philosophy of parenting: I may disappoint my parents with my actions, but nothing I do as their child will stop them from loving me.

To my parents, who are celebrating 42 years together, I say congrats. I love you more than you'll ever comprehend.

- 52 -

Antagonizing Your Spouse

I've got an amazing sister. 3 and a half years younger yet people always wondered if she was older than me. She's carried the hardworking genes of my parents into her life. An exceptional mother of 5. A nursing student. A wife of a police officer. There are very few that can match the resume that she carries.

Yet my most fond AND frustrating memories of our childhood together was how the both of us would antagonize each other. Isn't that what brothers and sisters do? We find ways to "egg on" our siblings into conflict by annoying them. The beauty of antagonizing them? They're the ones usually caught for being bad. We, the antagonizers, sit back and say, "What? I don't know why they're freaking out. I wasn't doing anything."

So immature. So childish. Yet, I see it so often amongst grown men and women living in holy matrimony. Some call it "egging their spouse on" into conflict. I call it "baiting" them. One spouse has become a silent predator baiting and setting their spouse up for disaster.

How does this happen? What does this look like?
Spouse #1 begins to antagonize Spouse #2. The moment happens and there's a subtle reaction...but all is still calm. Spouse #1 thinks, sets at bait, and the antagonizing continues. The pressure begins to build in Spouse #2, but the volcano is still dormant. The trap is reset again with more bait/antagonizing. This is it. The sleeping giant is awakened. The

pressure is released. Heated words are released into the atmosphere. Harsh tones with lined with verbal shrapnel fly through the air.

Spouse #1 gets to walk away telling friends, family, and/or the marriage counselor, "Spouse #2 has some anger issues. You should've seen what happened the other day." Spouse #1 then uses Spouse #2's responses as his/her excuse to step into unhealthy marital choices.

Being an avid sports fan, there's a term in hockey called the "retaliation penalty." You won't find it in the rule book. It's the term reserved for the guy who gets a penalty who is simple retaliating to the other player who was baiting him. It's childish. It's nothing more than a manipulation. We do things to get a reaction from our spouse that makes them look bad when it's really us seeding the poison into them. I've seen it happen. I've watched spouses antagonize in front of me. Yet I cannot say that I've never done that in my marriage. We are all susceptible to this.

Take a look at **Proverbs 4:23-27 (MSG):** <u>Keep vigilant watch over your heart</u>; that's where life starts. Don't talk out of both sides of your mouth; avoid careless banter, white lies, and gossip. Keep your eyes straight ahead; ignore all sideshow distractions. Watch your step, and the road will stretch out smooth before you. Look neither right nor left; <u>leave evil in the dust.</u>

I love the beginning and the end of this passage out of The Message. It speaks to this issue of being the antagonist in our marriage. "Keep vigilant watch over your heart...leave evil in the dust." The reality is, those that antagonize their spouse into fights and conflict have done the literal polar opposite. Their heart has become selfish. It's not about "how do we look good." It's about "how can I antagonize so that I LOOK GOOD."

It's time to grow up. It's time to throw off the childish games. It's time to apologize to our spouse for what we are doing (trust me...he/she knows what you're doing). Strive to watch your heart and leave evil in the dust. Make sure that your goal in marriage is to make the "we" look good and not just the "me."

I'd love to say that Rachael and I have grown out of antagonizing each other but that hasn't happened...and probably never will (as brothers and sisters normally don't). But if there's something that could be said of your marriage, let it be said that you and your spouse refuse to manipulate each other by antagonizing.

Today, keep watch over your heart. Leave evil in the dust.

- 53 -

"Silence is NOT Golden"
5 Helps When Silence
Hits Your Marriage

The question driving today blog: Is your heart for your marriage stronger than your silence?

Isaiah 62:1 (NASV), "For Zion's sake I will not keep silent, And for Jerusalem's sake I will not keep quiet, Until her righteousness goes forth like brightness, And her salvation like a torch that is burning."

Silence can be good. Small increments of silence are gifts. Whether it's for prayer or just to simply gather your thoughts, silence can be refreshing (especially if you have little ones...been there, bought the t-shirt, had a baby throw up on the t-shirt). You've heard the cliché, "Silence is golden." But strategic silence against your partner for the purpose of anger, resentment, and/or punishment is destructive. Hear this from the pro at the "silent treatment" (me).

Just the other day, Anne approached me on the subject. She's reading Jen Hatmaker's book, "For the Love" and gave me an amazing quote from Jen.

"Truthfulness hurts for a minute; silence is the kill-shot. My resentment built a stonewall; my voicing it began crumbling the divide."

It confirmed what I've come to see from my own life and years of working with couples: Strategic silence is deadly. So many couples are concerned about talking about certain subjects. Some are afraid to bring things up fearing the outcome. Ladies and gentlemen, this ought not to be. If you want to be healthy, don't be as concerned about the talked as you should be when the talking stops.

Here's a few practical thoughts:

1. **Suck up your stubbornness and break the silence!** The pain of speaking to an awkward or painful subject doesn't compare to what your silence is doing to your marriage. A silent issue does not equate to a solved issue. I liken it to a sliver. Just because it stopped bothering you, doesn't mean you shouldn't remove it. Waiting and/or ignoring just invites infection AND more pain than necessary.

2. **Make an appointment with your spouse!** It's so practical yet so overlooked. You both need to be position to give your undivided attention to the conversation without distractions. Your kids don't need to hear your conversation. Your friends and family don't need to be a part of your biz (this should be its own blog). Keep your social media "friends" out of it (another blog idea). Keep this between you two and have it done so that you can focus on the conversation.

3. **Don't get tired of breaching the same subject.** If I've heard it once, I've heard it a thousand times, "We've talked about this before." My admonishment: Don't stop. If you've dealt with it, then keep talking BUT change your approach. Restart the conversation but brainstorm a different solution. If that doesn't work, invite a Christ-centered counselor. Just don't stop the conversation because you think you're at an impasse. Calling it an "impasse" is pronouncing it "impossible." Don't give up hope. If you've got Christ AND a teachable heart, all things are possible.

4. **Taking a "time out" is healthy but doesn't end the conversation**. Time outs are good when tempers flare. Requesting one can be good for:
   - Relaxing and calming down.

- Doing something that will get you to decompress. Perhaps you ladies want to hit the speed bag or go for a fun. Maybe you guys want a bubble bath with Kenny G playing in the background.
- Remembering what is important.
- Praying for humility, patience, and wisdom.

NOTE: When the time out is done, resume the conversation. Just because you have decompressed, don't let the talk go back into silence. Resume and resolve.

5. **Remember: The priority isn't striving a personal win.** Humility and teamwork from both of you will pay huge dividends for your marriage. When selfishness and maliciousness are set aside, casualties are few and far between. Marital "wins" result in successes for the marriage itself. They're rarely one-sided. I say it so many times in premarital counseling, "A win for the 'we' is always a win for 'me.' But going after a win for 'me' isn't going to be a win for the 'we.'"

Isaiah 62:1 (NASV), "For Zion's sake I will not keep silent, And for Jerusalem's sake I will not keep quiet, Until her righteousness goes forth like brightness, And her salvation like a torch that is burning."

Victory, provision, blessing, and destiny for Israel were intrinsically connected to God's silence. They were a broken and lost nation. God had REPEATING reached out to them. Through prophets, the conversation was extended over and over. In my own flesh, I wondered why God put up with them. But out of His deep love for them, God refused to remain quiet. He knew his shattering the silence would revive the wayward nation giving them a new identity.

Is your heart for your marriage stronger than your silence? If you'll walk in humility, break the silence, you'll have an opportunity to speak victory, provision, blessing, and destiny into your marriage.

Step up. Speak up. Break the silence.

- 54 -

You're my partner not my project

I like to fix things.

I can't always say it fix things correct the first time. I wish I had the engineer mindset of my father or my grandfather possess. They had the ability to take anything apart and put it right back together. But I do my best. Typically, I'll google answers and watch the demonstration on YouTube. More often than not, the project does get done and Anne is very happy.

I'm not always in "fix it" mode but when I am, I'm ready to look for anything that needs to get done. I'll get into a zone and harness my "Tim 'the Tool Man' Taylor" mindset walking around looking for the next thing to fix. I don't care if it's a chip in the drywall or Anne's hair-straightener, I'm ready to attack.

This is where so many spouses get it wrong. We are never content with our spouse and he/she knows it. Good is never enough. We constantly see something that needs to be "fixed" with our spouse and, most people like this, have no problem letting their spouse know what's wrong with them. I'm not saying there's no legit issues that need to be taken care of. But I'm afraid we have too many homes where the spouse doesn't feel like a spouse. The spouse doesn't feel like a partner...

He/she feels like a project...nothing more than what is wrong in the home.

That may not be your intention, but it's the truth of what is happening. You are so bent on "fixing" what is broke in your spouse that you've forgotten that it's God's job to fix broken people.

What are the traits of a spouse who thinks they are married to project?

- **You know better.** Your way of life is superior and, obviously, your spouse isn't living up to that standard.
- **There's no equal footing.** Two full partners are not making up this marriage. You are the majority stockholder and your spouse is there as a silent partner. Decisions MUST go through you and ramifications follow if they don't.
- **You are the superhero and your spouse is the irrelevant side-kick.** You save the day and your spouse wonders why the sidekick is even necessary.
- **People don't hear anything good from you about your spouse.** When you refer to your spouse in conversations with friends, they can tell from the tone and the look on your face how discontented you are with him/her and they hear how you're going to change them.
- **You tend to talk to your spouse like a child.** Why not? He/she isn't as mature as you.
- **You make sure your kids know that you are the parent they should be coming to.** When you mention anything about your spouse to the kids, it's always in the sense of "they don't know better...let me tell you the right way of doing this."

I'm sure the list can continue, but the fact is we are ALL broken. We are all mistake ridden. Even as I type, I think of what the Psalms says,

"If you, LORD, kept a record of sins, Lord, who could stand?" Psalm 130:3 (NIV)

You drive to fix your spouse is proof enough that you need help just as much as he/she does. Stop trying to find fulfillment in fixing your spouse and find your fulfillment in Christ. Stop wielding conviction in the home when that is the job of the Holy Spirit to convict.

I like what Pete Briscoe says, be "intimate consultants. You are intimate because you know your spouse better than anyone else. And you are a consultant because you point your spouse in the right direction when asked." Remove the undo pressure and stress of the home and instead of trying to do something you don't have the ability to do, provide an atmosphere that fosters the presence of God. It's in His presence we find fullness. In in His presence, all of us are changed.

We're all broken but it's in Him we live and move and have our being.

- 55 -

"Beyond Words: 6 Ways to Express "I Love You" Without Words"

Once in awhile, I feel the need to write a disclaimer for a blog. This is one of those blogs.

DISCLAIMER: I believe in talking to each other. Communication is the oil of the engine of marriage. As it flows so does everything else. I DO NOT want you to stop talking to each other. Immature tactics like the "silent treatment" only go to further damage the marriage as it is pride-driven to injure your spouse in a futile attempt to hurt him/her more than they have hurt you.

Now that I got that out-of-the-way, the heart of today's blog is to help move "love" past words. I want you to learn to love without words. (You get that I don't want you to stop talking right?) I propose to you: if the gift of verbal communication between you and your spouse were to stop, what evidence would be left to convey the depth of your love?

It's what I love about the immense love of God that we are called to model. He wasn't afraid to tell His people of his love (Jeremiah 31:3 NLT). He wasn't afraid to express it (John 3:16 NLT).

Our culture seems to have watered down love to an emotion instead of a statement of our being; a flash of sentiment in our heart instead of a deep-seeded passionate conviction. And when we want to express it, 3 simple words are used (of which I do NOT take for granted): I love you. But I tend to wonder, in the day we live in, if those words have been muddied a bit.

Don't get me wrong. Please do not ever stop telling your spouse that you love them. The words "I love you" shouldn't be reserved just for special occasions. Being married IS a special occasion. Therefore, open up your mouth freely and frequently to express verbally your love (this is disclaimer #2).

But if you couldn't say it, specifically to him/her, what evidence would be left?

Your schedule.
What does your schedule convey to your spouse? Your calendar will speak vision. And vision is born out of passion. The priority of time and quality of moments will speak volumes about what you are passionate about. Share calendars and let your spouse see things from scheduled/blocked-off time together to vacations and down-time. I'm of a firm conviction that NO marriage should go a month without a date. It doesn't have to have immense cost (or any for that matter). But I've always said: consistent dates are cheaper than divorce lawyers.

Meaningful touches.
I read a study from UCLA several years ago that said that EVERY human being needs 8-10 meaningful touches a day to be healthy. But the key word there is "meaningful." What does that look like? For some of you with higher libido, it's learning how to touch your spouse non-sexually (simply put: a touch that isn't laced with expectations). For those who aren't driven physically, it's creating opportunities to impact your spouse with your touch. It's all about initiating creative touches that put aside your touch-agenda (or lack thereof) to create a healthy touch climate in your marriage that expresses your love for one another.

Self-initiated projects.

Are there things your spouse has been wanting to get done around the home? Are there projects that you hear him/her talk about frequently? This is as simple as making a mental note of what your spouse has been wanting to accomplish AND showing you took notice by scheduling and implementing that project. Whatever the task is, the love isn't conveyed in the actual project as much as it is in the action of listening and responding.

Special moments.

I'll admit, I don't like Hallmark created holidays. Also, I'm not big on gift giving (that's at the bottom of my love languages). BUT...it seems like the longer we're married, the more we take for granted special moments that either, come by the calendar, or by the nature of our relationship (anniversaries, birthdays, etc.). RECOGNIZING and/or CREATING significant moments helps your spouse feel more like your "significant other" rather than the "obligatory other."

Respect.

The absence of respect will kill the heart of a marriage. When a couple no longer recognizes the most base level of human dignity in one another, passion bleeds out and life leaves the relationship. Why? We respect what we value. It doesn't mean our spouse is going to always act in a respectable way. But do we value our marriage? If so, we need to be a spouse that works hard to live in a respectful way that shows how much we value, first the Lord, and then our spouse. When you lead in respect, you build hope. And where hope is present, love is grown.

How others perceive your spouse.

What is your spouse's reputation or image based upon your closest friends and/or coworkers? How do others perceive your spouse after they've interacted with you? Whether you like it or not, what you say or do will get back to your significant other (it always does). I've heard it said that "Integrity is who you are when no one is looking." Perhaps marital integrity is how much you love your husband/wife when he/she isn't around. What a statement of love to be a someone who hears that their spouse was speaking words of appreciation, gratitude, respect, and passion without them in the room.

Two challenges for you:

1. **Have a conversation with your spouse about this**. Ask your spouse what "non-verbal" ways speak out "I love you" to them. Get some input. Give some feedback. Perhaps, make some apologies where you (or both) have missed the mark. Marriage goals are not to point out where you lack; Marriage goals are to look to where you can grow.

2. **Make it a daily challenge.** On top of VERBALIZING the words "I love you," what can I do today to NON-VERBALLY express those words that will bless my spouse? Get personal and practical without the worry of reciprocation. This shows the true heart of a servant. And that is how marriage grows.

I'd love to say I've mastered this. To be honest, I think I have a ton of room for improvement. As a husband, one of the greatest privileges and challenges is to tell my wife I love her without uttering a single word. It's so simple yet not an easy task.

Sit with your spouse. Have the conversation with a vision of growing the communication of the commitment and love you both possess. Remember: marriage is a long-haul journey built within healthy daily moments of growth.

Love ya. Praying for you.

- 56 -

7 Habits of
Highly Defective Marriages: Part 1
"Spiritual Continuity"

Some years back, I had come across the famous book "7 Habits of Highly Effective People." It, to this day, is one of the most sold self-help books ever on the market. Since then there have been so many "spin-off" books that have spawned from the original. My personal favorite was the book "The 7 Habits of Highly Effective Teens: The Miniature Edition." Maybe it was because my life, at the time, was centered around reaching teenagers. I think it was more so about the size of the book. Reading hasn't always been my strong-point and I loved that it was short and to the point.

These last few chapters will be series of seven blogs designed to recognize unhealthy habits. If you're like me, I can get into read marriage blogs and think, "Communication, I communicate all the time" and I don't realize that my communication, even though it is being done, isn't being effective.

Habit #1: Spiritual Continuity con·ti·nu·i·ty ˌkäntn'(y)o͞oətē/ The unbroken and consistent existence or operation of something over a period of time.
Synonyms: continuousness, uninterruptedness, flow, progression

"Everyone then who hears these words of mine and does them will be like a wise man who built his house on the rock. And the rain fell, and the floods came, and the winds blew and beat on that house, but it did not fall, because it had been founded on the rock. And everyone who hears these words of mine and does not do them will be like a foolish man who built his house on the sand. And the rain fell, and the floods came, and the winds blew and beat against that house, and it fell, and great was the fall of it." Matthew 7:24-27 (ESV)

There could be no other #1 on this list.

This is that place where couples get things backwards. You don't get everything else in order and then, and only then, do you bring Christ into the picture. You don't build the house and THEN install the foundation. The foundation is first.
Highly defective marriages refuse to put Christ first.

"Well, my wife is the spiritual one. She's the one to bring God into the home." Struggling marriages have one of many things in common: one spouse is working at something that BOTH should be working together on. Are you the only one trying to bring Jesus into your marriage? If you are in a marriage like that, you are probably frustrated and fatigued. I don't have any easy answers for you other than "DON'T GIVE UP"!!!! I want to speak Galatians 6:9 into your life.

So let's not get tired of doing what is good. At just the right time we will reap a harvest of blessing if we don't give up.

There's no better time than now to tend to the foundation of your marriage. Here in Michigan, we've had an obscene amount of snow storms. Case in point...My mailbox:
The trouble is when the storm hits, people come to grips with how well they've built the home. Storms are not the time to build, they're time to rest in the comfort of what's established.

Build now. Set Christ as your foundation now. Help your marriage to keep from becoming defective.

- 57 -

7 Habits of
Highly Defective Marriages: Part 2
"Staying Single"

sin·gle, siNGgəl only one; not one of several
Synonym: one (only), sole, lone, solitary, by itself/oneself,
unaccompanied, alone

What therefore God has joined together, let not man separate. Mark
10:9 (ESV)

The synonyms of the word single say it all. People, who are married,
living by and for oneself. Daily life exists as if the marriage covenant
didn't even happen. "My spouse is an inconvenience." "I have a life
outside of my spouse." "My private life has nothing to do with my
married life."

Alone.

Single-mindedness in marriage causes corrosion to the integrity of the
marriage.
As said in so many sermons, blogs, books, etc., the design from the
beginning was "two becoming one." I'm not talking about the much-
needed time that men need to be with men and women need to be with
women. We all need time with friends. I enjoy time with the guys to
eat wings and watch football. Anne likes running and shopping with

her friends. I am talking about the intentional actions that individuals chase after to maintain a "single" life while being married. To claim to have a private life outside of the "two becoming one" means, quite simple, the two are NOT one.

To be single means to provide for one person.
To be single means there's no one to report
To be single means I'm responsible to myself and no one else.

In prison, there may be no worse punishment for prisoners (other than capital punishment). Solitary confinement causes an individual to breakdown on every level. One study (psychiatryonline.org) about solitary confinement says it can cause "hallucinations, and other changes in perception, as well as cognitive problems including memory loss, difficulty thinking, and impulsiveness." The more you isolate yourself away from your spouse, the more you abandon you spouse to "solitary confinement." By living single, you're inviting problems in marital perception, thinking, and impulsiveness that will break your unity down. Don't be surprised when you see this lifestyle cause jealousy, frustration, hurt, distrust, and resentment.

How else is your spouse supposed to act? You've put them in solitary confinement.
The relationship we have with God helps provide keys to starting, repairing, and maintaining a highly effective marriage. Why? I believe the image of God is shown in the covenant of marriage. There are so many parallels to take. One scriptures I'd like to speak into you:

James 4:8 (NLT), "Come close to God, and God will come close to you. Wash your hands, you sinners; purify your hearts, for your loyalty is divided between God and the world."
When we draw near to God, there is a reciprocal movement on his behalf. He comes near to us. The response we have to that closeness: humility and repentance so that our loyalty to our life outside of Him is severed.

It should be no different in our marriage. If you've been living single, draw near to your spouse. The only way to do that is to step away from being single. Approach your husband/wife in humility and repentance. If you've put them in "solitary confinement", there's gonna need to be some healing needed. But you step away and draw near so that the loyalty to your "singleness" can be severed and your marriage healed. Stop living single. Stop leaving your spouse in "solitary confinement."

Draw close to your spouse.

- 58 -

7 Habits of
Highly Defective Marriages: Part 3
"No Fun"

fun/fən/

noun: enjoyment, amusement, or lighthearted pleasure.

synonyms: enjoyment, entertainment, amusement, pleasure

adjective: amusing, entertaining, or enjoyable.

For everything there is a season, and a time for every matter under heaven: a time to be born, and a time to die; a time to plant, and a time to pluck up what is planted; a time to kill, and a time to heal; a time to break down, and a time to build up; a time to weep, and a time to laugh; a time to mourn, and a time to dance; a time to cast away stones, and a time to gather stones together; a time to embrace, and a time to refrain from embracing. Ecclesiastes 3:1-8 (ESV)

For a while, whenever I read that portion of scripture, my eyes went to the negative parts of the scripture. (Maybe that reveals something about my psyche...that would explain a lot). Focus gets drawn toward words like die, kill, break, weep, and mourn. We can get so caught up in theses inevitable unfortunates. Marriage is no different. We too can get drawn into "inevitable unfortunates" and dwell on them as if to forfeit the other side of the coin. It's time to get out of our marital pessimism. It's time to return to what we relished in our dating/courting.

Fun…times of enjoyment, amusement, or lighthearted pleasure. It's more than a noun (something to do). It should describe who you are (adjective).

Defective marriages struggle with a deficiency of fun. We treat our marriage like a business transaction instead of a growing relationship that THRIVES on fun. Couples forget that fun isn't optional for a growing marriage. It's a vital time filled with, according to our writer a time of building up, laughing, dancing, and embracing (which is my favorite one).

A couple of years ago, we had an odd winter here in Michigan. We hit temperatures in the 70's to the 80's. In the Michiganders minds, this was the best winter. It's as if we skipped the season of winter. The problem: it messed with our agriculture and was a tremendous burden for our farmers. Our harvest wasn't the same which affected our economy. Skipping a season may feel okay in the moment, but it's detrimental on so many deeper levels.

It may not seem like a huge deal, but I want you to know something: "FUN" is a marital season that is not optional. Skipping the season of fun in your marriage is detrimental on so many deep levels.

Come together with your spouse and plan out some fun. I'm not talking about what YOU think is fun. Look into your spouse's heart and position them for a great time. What do you two like to do together? What can you both do that will facilitate laughter, emotional intimacy, and stress-release? What can you two try that may be new? Have you talked with other couples to see what they do (get some ideas from others)?

Know this: marriage wasn't designed to be in a constant season of stale monotony. It's to reflect who God is. God is life. God is celebration. God is a God of enjoyment, amusement, or lighthearted pleasure. God is fun.

If our marriage is to reciprocate who He is, then our marriage, therefore, needs to have "fun." Don't just let it naturally happen. Be purposeful with your fun. Be strategic in your busyness. Be a fun spouse.

I leave you with a great scripture out of the Old Testament: Deuteronomy 12:7 (MSG) "Celebrate everything that you and your families have accomplished under the blessing of God, your God."

Get off your butt and go have a time of enjoyment, amusement, or lighthearted pleasure with your husband/wife...

Go have fun!

- 59 -

7 Habits of
Highly Defective Marriages: Part 4
"Criticism"

---

crit·i·cal/ kritikəl
adjective: expressing adverse or disapproving comments or judgments
Synonyms: disapproving, scathing, fault-finding, judgmental, negative

Don't pick on people, jump on their failures, criticize their faults—unless, of course, you want the same treatment. Don't condemn those who are down; that hardness can boomerang. Be easy on people; you'll find life a lot easier. Give away your life; you'll find life given back, but not merely given back—given back with bonus and blessing. Giving, not getting, is the way. Generosity begets generosity. Luke 6:37-38 (MSG)

Of all the ways there are to die (not that I'm looking for one), drowning has got to be ranked up there as one of the most miserable ways to go. Yet I find there are so many spouses drowning their spouse by flooding them with criticism.

You and your husband/wife have the ability to overwhelm each other with such critical (disapproving, scathing, fault-finding, judgmental, negative) words that it can cause an emotional shut-down. That emotional collapse can result in a detachment within your relationship. When one of you brings on a sudden barrage of criticism, you leave your spouse feeling shell-shocked. The results: disengagement and often, over time, leads to contempt.

Defective marriages have at least one individual that constantly speaks with a critical tongue. Criticism, if not handled is a form of emotional violence. It's used as an attack against the character of the other. The tongue is an open faucet that will beat down your spouse leave your partner broken down, gasping for emotional and mental "air." In most cases, they're going to be reaching out to something or someone for a fresh breath to breathe into them. What is sad is the breath they need should be coming from their spouse.

The Gottman Institutes says criticism is "a wish disguised...a negative expression of real need." What needs to be done is to shut off the valve of criticism and YOU take responsibility for change. Instead of unloading all blame, you begin to own the wish/need and help shoulder the responsibilities at hand. Critical spirits fractures the oneness between you and your spouse. Introspective and humble hearts heal and fortify your marriage.

According to Luke 6 in The Message, stop "picking on" your spouse with criticism. Shut off the valve. Give your marriage some air and let the introspection and humility breath life back into your marriage. If you do, watch life come back into the eyes of your husband/wife.

Stop being defective. Stop being so critical.

- 60 -

7 Habits of
Highly Defective Marriages: Part 5
"Inconsistent Sex"

in·con·sist·ent/inkən'sistənt
adjective: not staying the same throughout
Synonyms: unstable, irregular, unsteady, unsettled, uneven

The husband should fulfill his wife's sexual needs, and the wife should fulfill her husband's needs. The wife gives authority over her body to her husband, and the husband gives authority over his body to his wife. Do not deprive each other of sexual relations, unless you both agree to refrain from sexual intimacy for a limited time so you can give yourselves more completely to prayer. Afterward, you should come together again so that Satan won't be able to tempt you because of your lack of self-control. 1 Corinthians 7:3-5 (NLT)

The subject that people, single and marriage, have a hard time talking about but don't mind reading out is sex. When it comes to sex, it is the action that provides so much enjoyment yet so much conflict. The most common sexual conflict in marriage is in reference to frequency. In that average couple (not always the case) one spouse tends to have a higher libido and want more sex than the other. This leads the spouse with the higher sex drive to feeling underappreciated, unimportant, and unloved.

"Why doesn't my wife want me?"
"Why doesn't my husband desire me?"
"Why won't she initiate anything?"
"Why won't he touch me?"
This begins a spinning carousel of chaos where the other spouse thinks:
"Is sex all they want from me?"
"What about my love language?"
"I shouldn't have to do something I don't want."

It's at this place where it feels like the wheels are falling off. The carousal of sexual chaos is spinning and you don't know how to stop the cycle that continues to stifle the marital joy. Your marriage isn't the only one dealing with this. Couples struggle with sex being inconsistent (unstable, irregular, unsteady, unsettled, uneven). I'm not saying "inconsistent" as it is HAS TO HAPPEN on certain days at certain times. What I mean is your marital sex life has become irregular and unsteady. It's in a cycle of instability and frustration. It is vital to break this cycle that most couples fall into at one time or another.

There is no magic number. I'm not after getting you to the average frequency of the american couple. What I'm after is CONSISTENCY. What helps is remembering what 1 Corinthians 7 (NLT) tells us, "Do not deprive each other of sexual relations, unless you both agree"

I've never met a couple who had a consistent healthy sex life who wanted a divorce. But the act of depriving (deny a person the possession or use of something), has been used to destroy so many marriages. Let me clear the air on this: There is a difference between refusing occasionally and depriving someone habitually. If depriving has become your habit. You've let selfishness creep in. My wife says it best, "You are the only one that can meet the sexual needs of your spouse. No one else can. If you don't, you're opening up the door for the enemy to try to use someone else to fill in that need." (Anne is a wise woman.)

"Do not Deprive" simply means...

- Sexual intimacy is a God-given gift given to your marriage. To deprive your spouse is to deprive them of a gift from God
- Sex isn't a weapon to wield for power in the marriage. It cannot be used for leverage or manipulation.
- You are not after the minimum. You are just "doing your duty". You're after experiencing the gift TOGETHER. Sex connects us on three levels: physical, spiritual, and emotional... but that's for another blog
- You are after intimacy and not just release. It's not about releasing frustration. Sex is at the deepest level of intimacy and should be treated and enjoyed as such.

You have to start by taking your SELF off of it. It's recognizing that if you as a couple remove selfish needs and wants and walk in a manner that says, according to 1 Corinthians 7 (NLT), "your body belongs to me and mine belongs to you." I even love how the section ends. If you step away because you MUTUALLY decided to do it for a time, come together to make sure the enemy cannot tempt you at all.

The result of a consistent sex life is simple: It will be a mutually fulfilling sex life. It sounds easier on the blog that it is to be reality. But the beauty of it is it'll be more fun to practice than it will be to read. As I said earlier, I've never met a couple who had a consistent healthy sex life who wanted a divorce. Why? Because at the center of a consistent sex life, was a self-less, humble, servant-like heart.

And that makes for a HIGHLY EFFECTIVE marriage (and a fun one at that).

Stop being defective...
Stop being inconstant with your marital sex life...
Stop depriving and enjoy each other.

- 61 -

7 Habits of
Highly Defective Marriages: Part 6
"Lack of Laughter"

laugh·ter/laftər
noun: the action or sound of laughing
Synonyms: chuckling, chortling, guffawing, cackling, sniggering

I feel I can't blog on this topic enough. There are too many people who take themselves WAY TOO seriously. A great quote from Agnes Repplier says,

"We cannot really love anybody with whom we never laugh."

Such truth about a sorely forgotten VITAL aspect of marriage. We do not realize how necessary laughter is in marriage. Anne and I always talk (and blog) about our two essential ingredients to marriage: Jesus and laughter.

"Then our mouth was filled with laughter, and our tongue with shouts of joy; then they said among the nations, 'The Lord has done great things for them.'" Psalm 126:2 (ESV)

I remember it was almost four years ago, I was in the salon waiting for Anne to finish getting her hair cut. We were playful arguing back and forth about something silly. We were not just laughing; we were egging on each other causing a bit of a scene which drew in the rest of the people in the salon. We found out later (from Lisa...Anne's stylist) that after we left, the people in the salon (workers and customers) were talking about us. They assumed we had just gotten married because we were playful as well as willing to laugh so much together. Lisa blew them away when she told them married we had been married 15+ years. Why were they shocked at that? Because, for some reason, couples with any vintage, are NOT supposed to laugh that much.

Why do we see laughter as an option in marriage? Why do we not strive for more of it? We wait for it to happen like a desperate person holding their lotto ticket listening to the numbers being read on the TV. We yearn to laugh with our spouse again. We hope it'll happen. Maybe today we'll hit the jackpot and enjoy a time of fun together.

Laughter isn't something that happens randomly like a lightning strike. Laughter is fostered and cultivated. It has to be seen as an essential piece of the marriage puzzle. Take it from professionals. Comedian Bob Hope said laughter is an "instant vacation." Jay Leno says, "You can't stay mad at somebody who makes you laugh." And Bill Cosby says, "If you can find humor in anything, you can survive it." These men made a living on the understanding that laughing brings an astronomic affect to people. Crowds would gather around them to get "medicated" with humor (Prov. 17:22 NLT).

When it comes to laughter, it produces a number of benefits:

- Reduces stress and tension.
- Stimulates your immune system.
- An increase of natural painkillers in your blood.
- Reduces blood pressure.
- Raises your spirits.
- Laughter relieves tension and brings closeness.
- Having a sense of humor refreshes your relationship.

As you can see, laughter is not to be taken lightly. Laughter is to be indulged in. It's the dessert of life that should be enjoyed every day...as much as possible!!! You need this. Your spouse needs this. I want to help you increase the laughter and in your marriage. I challenge you to...

- Look for the "funny" in your day. Be aware of the humorous moments around you.
- Laugh when you don't feel like laughing.
- Make it a habit to share funny moments with your spouse. Don't wait to tell them later. Bring them into the moment.
- Become of student of your spouse. Study what makes them laugh.
- Reflect on funny times in your past together.

When it comes to laughing, psychologists and scientists agree. Their studies reveal that individuals who have a strong sense of humor are less likely to experience burnout and depression and they are more likely to enjoy life in general — including their marriage.

Do you want a marriage that is set up for success? Do you want to bring health and vitality to your marriage? Do you want a marriage that is HIGHLY EFFECTIVE?

Create a culture of laughter.

- 62 -

7 Habits of
Highly Defective Marriages: Part 7
"Curdled Heart"

cur·dle/ˈkərdl
verb: To separate or cause to separate into curds or lumps. To spoil or turn sour.
Synonyms: clot, coagulate, congeal, thicken

And she was in bitterness of soul, and prayed unto the LORD, and wept sore. 1 Samuel 1:10 (KJV)

Bitterness, to many people, is the most sensitive of the tastes. Most of us find it harsh and unpleasant. My case in point: Unsweetened cocoa. I remembered discovering it in our pantry growing up. To me, it looked like chocolate. To my chagrin, my mouth was filled with the shockingly harsh taste of unsweetened cocoa. It blew my mind that anything bearing the brown Hershey label could taste so bad! It cured me of sneaking around to find chocolate...well, almost.

Identifying bitterness is not as simple as a taste test. A harsh or bitter person will rarely admit it. He/she will call themselves firm, melancholy, sober, principled or any number of pseudonyms for bitter. Here's the reality: bitterness is very easy to see in others but hard to see in ourselves. It sits in our heart releasing its venom causing the curdling process to begin. Over time the bitterness begins to spoil our attitude.

Our personality begins to sour and our defenses begin to thicken. If not taken care of, bitterness turns to unforgiveness and causes hearts to separate.

Bitterness has now finished its work.

Defective marriages hold onto the toxin of bitterness, anger, and regret? I say quite often, unforgiveness (which comes from bitterness) is the cancer of marriage. And as a pastor, I deal with this issue more than most. Bitterness will break apart/curdle your heart and undermine your marriage.

In 1 Samuel 1 (KJV), we find the scripture talking about someone in agony. The "she" being talked about is a woman named Hannah. She was hurting. She was broken. And yes, she was bitter. Unable to conceive, she was in inner turmoil. The Hebrew word for "bitterness" means bitter taste or inner pain. She was experiencing both. We have limited knowledge to what was taking place here in 1 Samuel 1 (KJV). But we cannot help but speculate that her bitterness was taking its toll on her personally as well as her marriage.

The story is kept simple. And even though we only need 10 verses to see Hannah's agony. We only need a few words to see her response to the bitterness.
Hannah turned to the Lord.

It may sound like a religious cop-out, but something far deeper was happening than a religious crutch. She was emptying her burden/bitterness upon the shoulders of God. It wasn't for a moment of release. It says in verse 12 (KJV), she "continued praying before the Lord." She refused to live in bitterness. She didn't succumb to its venom. Hannah didn't play games with it. She opened up, faced it, and cried out to the Lord for help.

There is a beauty to the simplicity of Hannah's response. Bitterness wants to isolate you and curdle your heart toward your spouse, yourself, and the Lord. It wants to do its work of separation. But if we, simply, opened up to face it head on, we'd see that bitterness is normal for us to face but abnormal for us to carry. Your shoulders where never built to hold it.

One of my favorite scriptures says this:

Cast your burden on the LORD, and he will sustain you. Psalm 55:22 (ESV)

Are you harboring bitterness? Have you succumbed to its venomous hold? Has your heart started curdling toward your spouse? Then do yourself and your marriage a favor.
In bitterness of soul...cast your burden on the Lord. And if you will, his promise is he will sustain you.

For Hannah, God gave her a son Samuel that would bless a nation. For you, I do not know what God has planned, but I believe though you, God will birth great things that will bless the world around you.

Stop feeding the defectives of marriage.
Stop being bitter.
Cast your burden on the Lord.

ABOUT THE AUTHOR

David Barringer, currently the lead pastor of Kalamazoo First Assembly of God, earned a bachelor's degree from Central Bible College. He is a blogger at pdave.me, which includes his Friday marriage ramblings. He and his wife, Anne, have two children and live in Kalamazoo, Michigan.